"…In Defence of Her Honor"

THE TILLIE SMITH MURDER CASE

With best wishes –

[signature]

Saturday, December 15, 2001

More than 100 participants took the "Tillie Walk" produced by the Centenary Stage Company during Hackettstown's Chocolate Festival. The walk, retracing the steps of Tillie Smith on her last night alive, was led by costumed guides Douglas Steinberg, left in top hat, and Megan O'Toole, right in cape. Denis Sullivan, who wrote "In Defense of Her Honor" about Ms. Smith's 1886 murder, assisted.

"...In Defence of Her Honor"

THE TILLIE SMITH MURDER CASE

by Denis Sullivan

D. H. Moreau Books

FLEMINGTON, NEW JERSEY

For information about permission
to reproduce selections from this book, write to:
Jay Langley, Executive Editor
D.H. Moreau Books
P.O. Box 32, Flemington, N.J. 08822-0032

Book design by Catherine Langley

Library of Congress Cataloguing-in-Publication Data
Sullivan, Denis, 1938–
In defence of her honor / Denis Sullivan
192 p.   cm.
Includes bibliographical references
ISBN 0-9662789-3-3

First Edition – 2000
Printed in the United States of America

D.H. Moreau Books
18 Minneakoning Road • P.O. Box 32 • Flemington, N.J. 08822-0032

To Joan, Lisa and Karen

List of Illustrations

Tillie Smith Monument, Union Cemetery, Hackettstown, N. J.

Courtesy of Betty Jo King

Preface

Tillie Smith lies at the top of a hill in Union Cemetery at the eastern edge of Hackettstown, near the border of Morris and Warren counties in New Jersey. Beyond the cemetery's triple-arched stone gateway is a macadam strip. Once a rutted wagon path bordered by tall trees, it runs about 50 yards to the Musconetcong River and crosses by an iron bridge whose floorboards rumble ominously under the weight of even the smallest cars. The river is the county line. On the opposite bank, where the burial ground begins, the road narrows and winds its way upward past small and large family plots, modest slate headstones and handsome polished granite obelisks. Tillie's monument, an elegant work in high relief on a 7-foot granite slab, stands atop a double-tiered pedestal on Crest Drive, the cemetery's highest elevation. It depicts a maiden in classical robes, graceful and supple as a dancer, balancing delicately on her right foot, her left knee resting on a narrow background ledge. Her left hand grasps the slab's rough face for purchase as she reaches upward with her right to place a laurel crown above a tablet. There is an epitaph on the tablet, in raised letters: "She died in defence of her honor, April 8, 1886, aged 18 years," it says, with an added proclamation that the monument was "erected by an appreciative public."

I first saw it in the fall of 1984, shortly after relocating to Karrsville, a few miles from Hackettstown. Some errand or other had taken me past the old cemetery late one afternoon. Out of curiosity, I wandered through the gate and eventually reached the crest of the hill where the granite maiden stood on her double pedestal. The afternoon sunlight accentuated the contrast of her smooth curves with the roughness of the background slab. It was late October; the ground was covered with dry leaves, and the wind had raised a pile of them against one side of the pedestal, nearly burying a small cross left by another visitor. A burned-out votive candle in a small glass lay beside it. I picked up the cross and examined it, turning it over and over. It was made of twigs whose edges had been neatly trimmed, a string joining them tied with great care in an intricate diamond pattern. The sun cast the maiden's shadow partially across the side of the tablet next to her, and her epitaph stood out boldly. Its archaic spelling expressed an archaic sentiment, yet the monument's ability to grip the viewer could not be denied, nor could its intimation of causes worth dying for and meanings to be found in hard deaths that come too soon. Even today's public, from whom expressions of appreciation for heroic virtue are rare, would be hard put to dismiss such a memorial as mere Victorian sentimentalism.

Who was Tillie Smith, and why had she earned immortality in her day?

The light was fading and there was a distinct chill in the air as I began walking back down the path. I took a final look back at the granite maiden and the shadows deepening around her, and I promised myself I'd learn her story some day.

In the years that followed, articles about Tillie Smith appeared occasionally in local newspapers. I read them all. Some were fanciful (as in Halloween accounts of ghostly appearances at Hackettstown's Centenary College) and none was detailed enough to satisfy my curiosity. Finally, I decided to do my own research, and went back to the original newspaper accounts. One week later, after working my way through microfilmed editions of *The New York Times*, *Washington Star*, *Belvidere Apollo*, *Hackettstown Gazette* and *Warren Republican* at the public library in Belvidere, I had a bare outline of the events that had made Tillie Smith a local historical figure, and even more questions than when I began. And I was hooked.

Tillie (nobody seems to have called her by the more formal Matilda except in official documents) was born in poverty and raised in a broken home. She was barely literate. She died where she worked as a kitchen maid, so the stories went, at Hackettstown's Centenary Collegiate Institute, raped and strangled in one of its vault-like basement chambers. She had last been seen alive inside the Institute grounds after returning from a variety show in Hackettstown, shortly after 10 p.m. Her body, discarded in a nearby field, was found early the next morning. No one knew if she had even reached the servants' entrance in the rear of the Institute's basement that night, but one of her co-workers, the janitor who would normally have let her into the building after hours, became the prime suspect.

Although he insisted that the victim never came to the servants' door while he was on duty, investigative reporters from several New York City daily newspapers spun a circumstantial case around him. He was tried, convicted of first-degree murder and sentenced to death. His date with the hangman barely three weeks off, all appeals having failed, he confessed to committing the crime in circumstances amounting to second-degree murder. In return for this admission his death sentence was commuted to life imprisonment at hard labor. He was whisked off to the state's grim penitentiary in Trenton before the public could take matters into its own hands — that same "appreciative public" that acknowledged the victim's gallantry later that year by erecting an impressive memorial to her at the crest of the town cemetery's only hill. Case closed.

Well, not quite. More than a century later, some very troublesome questions are still unresolved. Was the janitor really guilty, or a victim of overzealous prosecutors and sensational journalism? There were negative references in local newspapers to the aggressiveness with which members of the New York press supposedly solved the crime.[1]

Did they manufacture a circumstantial case to increase their papers' circulation?

Did Tillie Smith's apotheosis and the suspect's vilification in their pages, day after day, make conviction a foregone conclusion?

There is the issue of the Chief Justice of the Criminal Court: He presided at the trial, and was afterward made a justice of the New Jersey Supreme Court. In that capacity he not only heard the janitor's appeal, but sustained his own rulings from the lower court. Should he not have disqualified himself?

There is the question of the genuineness of the janitor's confession, which differed in important details from the evidence developed during the trial. Many townspeople, especially the champions of Tillie Smith's death "in defence of her honor," dismissed it as a fabrication, a desperate maneuver by the attorneys to save their client's neck. But the authorities appear to have accepted it without question. Why would the prosecutors even consider, let alone accept, what amounted to an after-the-fact plea bargain when the defendant had already been tried, convicted and sentenced to death? Why, when they had gone to exceptional lengths to establish his premeditation and malice circumstantially?

And this: On his release from prison at the end of 1904, the janitor returned to Hackettstown to spend the remainder of his life — nearly half a century — among the very people who had seriously considered lynching him only 18 years before. Why?

This book attempts to find the answers and tell the entire story in a historically accurate way. To do this, however, requires that we put aside any nostalgia we may have for an imagined better life in the "good old days," and take a hard look at the crime in its rural 19th-century New Jersey setting. For all the romanticizing of Victoriana, the fact is that the period had a dark and sinister aspect that can't be ignored. Conditions in New Jersey's interior may never have approached the squalor of London's Whitechapel or its American counterpart, New York City's Five Points, but there was no immunity to be had from brutal crime and hard living conditions. Rural New Jersey in the 1880s had its share of social ills, and local newspapers of the period attest to murder, rape, assault, robbery and assorted misdemeanors.[2] To these must be added deaths in railroad accidents, maiming by crude industrial and agricultural machinery, disease, and complications of childbirth.

If the Warren County Court's docket books of the period are any indication, saloons and brothels appear not only to have outnumbered churches but to have been better attended. It was grand to be alive in late Victorian New Jersey if one had wealth and social standing. If one had neither, life was more likely to fit the Hobbesian paradigm: nasty, brutish and, with unfortunate frequency, brief.

The newspaper was the principal medium of that day. Its supporting technologies — telegraphy; high-speed, high-volume printing; and rail transportation — were well enough developed by the 1880s that residents of New Jersey were able to enjoy their favorite New York City dailies within hours of printing. National and regional news was obtained from *The New York Times*, *The World*, *The Tribune*, *The Herald*, *The Telegram*, *The Sun*, and a host of other journals less famous but, with the exception of the first-named, equally long-dead. Local journals, usually published weekly, were the sources of political, social and religious news in the smaller towns. For those in search of titillation, magazines such as *National Police Gazette* were the *National Enquirers* of their day. Because of the spectacular nature of the Tillie Smith case — rape and murder at a Methodist seminary — all of them gave the story extensive coverage.[3] The affair ultimately became a media circus, as correspondents flooded Hackettstown and the dailies vied with each other to present more and more lurid and sensational accounts of the crime, investigation and trial.

Events in Hackettstown during the spring of 1886 suggest that the town's administration and its leading citizens were highly sensitive to criticism by the big city press and, consequently, eager to accommodate its representatives. The urban daily newspapers were instrumental in goading the Hackettstown Common Council to offer a reward, and in motivating otherwise frugal townspeople to subscribe generously to an expensive monument.

Worse, it appears that they were able to convince police investigators to abandon some leads in favor of others which they thought were more promising. The ability of the metropolitan newspapers to hold an entire population up to ridicule as "rubes" and "yokels" before hundreds of thousands of readers, day after day, appears to have been pivotal. Few small-town administrations can withstand negative attention on a grand scale, and Hackettstown's caved in to aggressive investigative reporters almost immediately. Left to break the case in their own way, the gentlemen of the press examined and analyzed it in minute — if not always accurate — detail in their pages, focusing their suspicions on the janitor so relentlessly that his eventual conviction was almost anticlimactic.

So many reporters covered the case, and so intense was their rivalry in that era of freewheeling journalism, that "exclusive" interviews with the principal witnesses, the victim's family, and even the accused himself appeared in nearly every edition.[4] Circulation may have received a significant boost; sadly, we cannot say the same for due process.

It is said that at Joseph Pulitzer's *World* a sign exhorted reporters to "get facts, facts, facts." This may have been true, but it appears to have had very little influence on dispatches from *The World's* reporter in Hackettstown. Nor was Pulitzer's competition much better. Today's press, a frequent target of allegations of bias, inaccuracy and hyperbole by people who long for the "good old days" is a model of probity compared with its 19th-century ancestors.

In the Tillie Smith case, publications rarely agreed except in the broadest depiction of events, and even verbatim testimony varied from one to the next. Some reporters, it appears, were not beyond embellishing facts, or simply inventing them if the need arose. Important detail, especially forensic evidence, was omitted from the accounts altogether because it was considered unfit for publication under editorial standards of the day. Thus, anything but the most limited use of those accounts as source material was problematic if there was no separate corroboration.

Corroboration can usually be found in official documents: police reports, records of autopsies and inquests, indictments, photographic exhibits, maps, letters, and, especially, transcripts of trials and records of appeals. These provide a factual basis for an account, while permitting evaluation of individual newspapers' credibility.

Unfortunately, nearly all of the Tillie Smith case records were impossible to obtain locally. Warren County lacks a formal archive. The county Prosecutor's office reported that it held no grand jury records dating before the 1940s, and records of coroners' inquests from the 1880s appear to have been consigned to a trash bin when the county courthouse was renovated in the 1950s.

As for the transcript of the trial, which could be expected to contain references to both inquest and grand jury testimony, several local authorities expressed doubt that one had even been produced. The sum of Warren County's records of the case amounted to some chronological records of the court proceedings, including jury selection, the order of testimony at trial, motions and sentencing. Interesting, but of no great substance.

Brian Smith, a Warren County attorney with an interest in local history, assured me that a transcript must have been produced because the New Jersey courts of 1886 used stenographers and typewriters. Further research proved him correct. A *New York Times* article written toward the close of the trial contained this bit of information: "(t)he evidence is very voluminous, covering 1,500 pages of printed matter. Each attorney is provided with a copy and frequently consults the contents."[5] The last few lines of a second *Times* article published three days later mentioned the cost of the trial, and reported: "The legal stenographers will receive $600."[6] And an itemized account of the cost of the trial appearing afterward in the Washington, N.J., *Star* contained entries totaling nearly $1,000 for the services of "Knight & Grichtel [sic], Stenographers."[7]

While this established beyond any doubt that transcripts had been produced, finding one of them more than a century later was another matter. Attorney Smith, by coincidence, occupied the former law offices of J.G. Shipman & Son, the defendant's counsel. He was kind enough to look through old case records there in the hope of locating the Shipmans' own copy of the transcript, but found that the oldest records on hand went back only to the 1920s. Some Shipman descendants still living in the area were located and interviewed, but none knew the whereabouts of the law office's older files. Things were looking bleak until I mentioned to attorney Smith that I had found an appellate report of the case in the county law library. He thought about that for a moment, and then suggested I check in the state Capitol. His reasoning was that since appeals require submission of the record from the court below, a transcript might still be on file in the Appellate Division.

I went to Trenton a few days later and requested a record search at the State Archive. Within minutes an archivist located the very transcript filed with the appeal, a compendium of 1,506 pages, some original typewritten sheets and some carbon copies, with the name "Knight & Gnichtel" printed in red at the top of each. After gathering dust in the state Supreme Court's files for more than 80 years, it had been hardbound in two volumes and placed in the state library's rare book collection. I had struck gold!

It's difficult to describe the pleasure of opening those volumes for the first time, except to suggest imagining what Howard Carter might have felt as he responded to the question, while shining his light through a chink in the wall of King Tut's tomb, whether he could see anything. "Wonderful things!" he replied.

Wonderful things indeed: I discovered forensic evidence that had been considered unfit to print, important bits and pieces of evidence that reporters thought too insignificant to include in their accounts, and even the court's charge to the jury.

Sadly, four pages of testimony by one witness and three pages of another's had been excised from the middle of volume one, with only the Q's and A's of the stenographer's record remaining visible near the left-hand margins. And, to my disappointment, none of the opening statements of counsel and only part of one of the four closing statements (that of the prosecutor) had been included in the transcription.

On the positive side, the pages were in excellent condition, and the testimony of all the other witnesses was complete and legible. The characters in the drama suddenly came alive as each page revealed their actual words. They were easily imagined in the witness chair, providing testimony that would mean life or death for the defendant.

You will soon be reading some of it yourself. Now, imagine yourself seated in the jury box as their testimony is presented. You will decide: Is the defendant a rapist and a murderer, or an innocent victim of circumstance? Are the witnesses against him credible? Could the crime have occurred as the prosecution says it did, or are other scenarios as likely? Does the prosecution's evidence prove the defendant's guilt beyond a reasonable doubt?

And when you've answered those questions to your satisfaction, ask yourself another: whether this story of crime and punishment will give you pause if ever again you are tempted to view the late 19th century through a scrim of nostalgia for things Victorian, or to long for so-called kinder, gentler times.

Acknowledgements

I am indebted to a number of people.

First, the late Marion Goeller Freeman, James Titus' granddaughter and only remaining relative, who graciously consented to be interviewed, and her minister, Dr. Frank Fowler III of Trinity United Methodist Church, Hackettstown.

Also, Janet Davis, reference librarian at the Warren County Public Library's main branch in Belvidere; Robert Lupp, rare books librarian at the New Jersey State Library in Trenton; New Jersey State Archivist Bette Epstein; and Warren County Clerk Terry Lee.

The encouragement of attorney Brian Smith of Belvidere was greatly appreciated, not to mention his patience with my fledgling legal research. Betty Jo King provided many of the illustrations from her incomparable collection of historic Warren County photographs, and Centenary College's Simone Knaap and Carol Bodrogi made material from the college archives available. Special thanks, also, to Meg Bellinger and Carmen Howard of Preservation Resources, Bethlehem, Pa., for their high-quality microfilm of the trial transcript; the Hackettstown Historical Society; the Methodist Archives at Drew University; the reference librarians of the Phillipsburg Free Public Library; and my publisher Jay Langley, at D. H. Moreau Books, the book division of the Hunterdon County Democrat newspaper company in Flemington, N.J.

And last, but not least, my wife Joan, who helped find source documents in a hot dusty attic, read and re-read innumerable drafts and, in her gentle way, removed the wind from my prose without removing it from my sails.

D.S.
Karrsville, N.J.

"The combination of sex, violence and the deplorable insubordination of the lower classes was most attractive to the journalists of the day."

From *Alias Grace*, referring to the Kinnear-Montgomery murders, which took place in 1843 in Canada, and which were extensively reported by the press in Canada, the United States and Great Britain.

Margaret Atwood

"Truth is the daughter of time."

Francis Bacon

"…In Defence of Her Honor"
THE TILLIE SMITH MURDER CASE

Chapter One

The monument to chastity, in whose cause Tillie Smith is said to have given her life, keeps a lonely vigil at the summit of the only hill in Hackettstown's Union Cemetery. It stands in the most prominent place of all in an area once reserved for the community *gratin*. Within sight of it, in a small family plot a short distance down the slope, a simpler stone bears the names of James Johnson Titus and the generations of his family. On another hill, barely a mile away, Centenary College's Seay Hall, its once-shiny copper dome now covered in a rich, green patina, towers above many of the same trees that surrounded its Victorian Gothic predecessor, Centenary Collegiate Institute.

Tillie Smith, a domestic who lived and worked there, was raped and strangled — some say inside the darkened passages of the old Institute's basement, others say in a nearby outbuilding — one chilly April night more than a century ago. Her body was left in plain view in an open field, in a far corner of the campus where the college library now stands.

In the weeks that followed, Titus, a highly respected resident of the town and fellow employee of the victim, became ensnared in a web of circumstantial evidence that led to his arrest and indictment. In October 1886, he was convicted of rape and murder, and sentenced to hang.

Situated in the Musconetcong Valley at the eastern edge of Warren County, Hackettstown came to maturity in the decades following the Civil War. By 1886, the Morris Canal, an early 19th-century engineering marvel which marked the town's western border and contributed much to its initial wealth, had already begun losing business to the state's growing network of rail lines.[1] There was little concern in Hackettstown, though: The Delaware, Lackawanna & Western Railroad's new terminal and yards on Valentine Street, just below the old canal route, gave visible assurance of cheap and convenient transportation to the ma-

American House Hotel, Hackettstown, N.J.

Centenary Collegiate Institute, Hackettstown, N.J.

chinery and carriage manufacturers that were the backbone of its growing economy.

The town's streets and lanes were still unlit, and most were unpaved, but its major thoroughfare was relatively broad and tree-lined, and boasted an ornate two-story post office and two fair-sized hotels. The American House, at the uptown end of Main Street nearer the railroad depot, catered to business travelers and "drummers" (as salesmen were then called). Warren House, about a half-mile away at the opposite end of Main, was regarded as the better of the two, an upscale family establishment.

Two blocks downtown from the American House, on the same side of Main Street, was Trinity Methodist Church, its slender, white steeple rising far above the neighboring shops and houses. The New England-style clapboard building was the second church of that name to occupy the site, and would be razed the following year to be replaced by one more impressive if less graceful, made of brick.

To one side of the post office, directly across the street from the church, where a number of lots had once stood vacant, a new plank-covered lane had been cut through a distance of four blocks to connect Main and Jefferson streets. Church Street, as the new lane was called, began opposite the front door of Trinity Methodist Church and ended opposite the wrought-iron front gate of Centenary Collegiate Institute, the town's new junior college and Methodist seminary. The church, the Institute and the new corridor connecting them straddled the center of town like a large letter H, giving notice to all that in this place Methodism was a power to be reckoned with.

Centenary Collegiate Institute, Centenary College's predecessor, was a massive structure. Its dull brick, brownstone trim and iron-railed mansard roof gave it more the appearance of an asylum than an educational institution. Popularly known as "the Seminary," "the Institute," and sometimes simply by its initials "CCI," it was a source of great local pride. The town directory, newspapers and other publications in which advertisements for it appeared never failed either to show an engraving of its Gothic

Courtesy of Centenary College

Centenary Collegiate Institute viewed from the Jefferson Street gate, as it appeared at the time of the murder. The window from which Arturo Rivera and Harry Smith saw Tillie and Munnich is the second dormer from the right.

outer skin or make mention of the modern engineering amenities which lay beneath it.[2]

Contemporary taste may dismiss the old Institute's somber features as ponderous and overdone, but in its day it was one of the area's great attractions and its history is worthy of mention. In 1867, the Newark Conference of the Methodist Episcopal Church celebrated the centennial of Methodism in America by announcing it would build a higher education facility in northern New Jersey. A number of town and cities, all larger and closer to Newark than Hackettstown, were included on the Conference's list of possible sites. Hackettstown's community leaders offered the Conference a lucrative package — a 10-acre tract bounded by First Avenue, Plane, Moore and Jefferson streets, plus $10,000 in cash — as an inducement to locate the new facility there. The proposal had the additional advantage of being strongly supported by two members of the decision-making body who were residents. It was accepted, and the cornerstone of Centenary Collegiate Institute's main building was laid near the Jefferson Street side of the site on September 9, 1869. The Conference's policy was to build without incurring substantial debt, thus construction was sporadic and took five years. With the help of innumerable fundraising drives — including at least one mid-winter dinner in the building's unfinished and unheated dining hall — the impressive Victorian Gothic structure was eventually completed.

More than 100 feet tall and 220 feet wide, and nearly 50 feet deep, it was by far the largest building in town. There were dining and reception rooms, a chapel, men's and women's dormitories, and the most modern amenities then available: steam heat, hot and cold running water, and bathrooms on every floor. A three-story extension protruding more than 100 feet from the building's center rear housed a kitchen, utility rooms and classrooms, and an elaborate trapezoidal clock tower with an ornamental railing at its top straddled the mansard roof. The tower gave the Institute the distinction of being the tallest, if not necessarily the best-looking, structure in the area. Its chiming clock, a gift from Hackettstown, could be heard from one end of town to the other.[3]

Reverend George H. Whitney, D.D.

Front lawn of Centenary Collegiate Institute showing a bit more of what Arturo Rivera and Harry Smith could have seen.

Centenary's doors opened in September 1874 at an inaugural ceremony attended by more than 5,000 people. Its first president, Rev. George H. Whitney (a distant relative of inventor Eli Whitney), was a capable leader. Under his administration, the coeducational Institute soon became an important and influential feature of the village.

During the 1880s, male and female students and staff living on campus accounted for nearly 7 percent of Hackettstown's population,[4] while other employees — such as James Titus — who maintained homes in town, increased the ratio. The very size of the Institute was bound to have an effect on town affairs, and among the inevitable town-gown disputes were unfounded accusations by tavern owners and innkeepers that the Institute's "dry" seminarians were using their voting influence to block the granting of new liquor licenses.[5]

However, the prestige that comes of playing host to a distinguished school seems to have weighed far more heavily than the occasional conflict, and most townspeople seem to have thought well of the Institute and its students.

As can be imagined, the discovery on its grounds of one of its employees, strangled and apparently raped, was doubly shocking: The Institute's religious affiliation and the tranquil beauty of the surroundings seemed to make it an unlikely setting for so brutal a crime.

Thursday, April 8, 1886, was typical of early spring. A chilly rain had fallen earlier in the day, and by late afternoon the skies were still partly cloudy, the temperature falling rapidly toward freezing.[6] As daylight faded and the short stretch of the Morris Canal along the base of Buck Hill at Hackettstown's western limit was lost in deepening shadows, the last few stragglers could be seen coming in from the fields surrounding the Institute's 10-acre campus. Despite the possibility of late snowfalls, plowing and sowing had begun. By sunset, the sky finally cleared. The moon, not yet in its first quarter, was about four hours from setting.[7] Soon the darkness was complete, save for the gas-lit Institute grounds, and pinpoints of light in doorlamps and windows of nearby houses.

The only known photograph of Tillie Smith.

Shortly before 7:30 p.m., a young woman emerged from the seminary's wrought iron front gate and crossed Jefferson Street.[8] Eighteen-year-old Tillie Smith had lived in and around Hacketts-town for more than a year, and was adventurous enough to know her way around its streets and lanes at all hours. Born in Water-loo, N.J., she lived there with her father and two younger siblings after her parents' separation eight years earlier. The previous Oc-tober, she had moved to Hackettstown to be nearer the farm on which her mother worked as a domestic.

A photograph, probably taken only a few months before her death, shows the slightly plump and pretty-faced teenager in a studio pose of the period, standing in front of a painted pastoral backdrop, wearing a fancy floral hat, her right hand draped casu-ally over a prop of a country fence. Her gaze is focused slightly above and behind the lens. There is a wistful, almost melancholy aura about her, as if she were looking toward a clouded and un-certain future.

After short-term employment in two or three agricultural households, she had come to work for the family of Dr. William Conover, who lived in the woods on the outskirts of Hacketts-town. The doctor would later testify how impressed he was by his servant's fearlessness, recalling that she would go into town and return home after dark, walking along deserted country roads without the least hesitation.[9]

It appears that Tillie, who had no formal education, was an eager learner, because the doctor taught her to read during her brief employment. She left the Conovers at the end of 1885, and was hired by the Institute as a potato peeler the following month. Her employment there was unremarkable. The matron and fellow workers regarded her as quiet, proper and reliable.[10]

April in northwest New Jersey is notoriously unpredictable, and deceptively mild spring afternoons frequently give way to cold temperatures an hour or two after sunset. Tillie was dressed for the weather that evening: A heavy cloak covered her brown woolen dress and gray jacket; beneath the dress were several pet-ticoats and two pairs of drawers, one of flannel and one of muslin;[11] her shoes were almost new; and a flowered hat, new kid

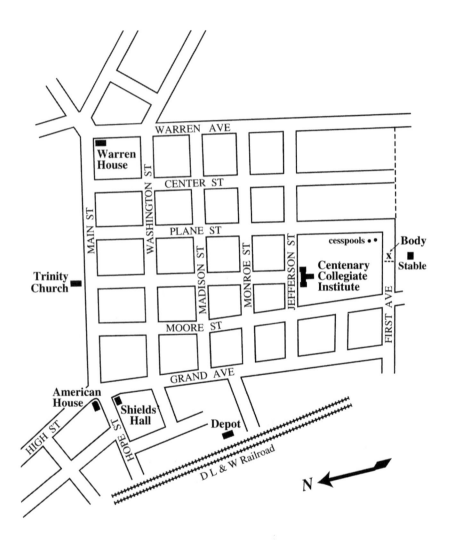

Central Hackettstown

c.1886

gloves and a small red purse completed her outfit. The purse contained between six and seven dollars in bills and assorted coins, as she planned to do some shopping before attending a local variety show.[12]

Once across Jefferson Street, she began walking up Church Street toward Main, perhaps wondering whether the evening's plans would get her into trouble for violating the Institute's 10 o'-clock curfew. She was a new employee, and the only other time she had asked for permission to come in after 10 o'clock the matron, Elizabeth Ruckle, had refused.[13]

At around six that evening, she had encountered janitor James Titus in the dining room, where he was having supper before starting his night shift. She told him of her plan to go into town, adding that she would probably come in after curfew and would need to enter through the basement without the matron's permission.[14]

Titus hadn't liked the idea. Twenty-nine years old, he had worked at the Institute almost from the day it opened, and his janitor's title belied the responsibility of the position to which he had risen during 11 years of conscientious service. He tended the furnaces, did minor cleaning and repairs, and directed a battery of domestics. There were important administrative responsibilities, too, including estimating construction and repair work, and purchasing materials and supplies. He also served as night watchman, with responsibility for securing the entire building after lights-out, making rounds, and reporting the names of students or servants who came in after curfew without permission.[15]

The Institute was very strict with the female servants, and required that they obtain written permission from the matron to come in after 10 p.m. It should not have surprised Tillie, a new employee, that Titus refused to help her violate this rule. She was insistent, though; when he suggested that she go ask the matron, she became indignant and told him that she'd sooner spend the entire night out than be refused permission again. Titus thought she was joking, and returned to his supper.[16] A little more than an hour later, she walked out into the darkness.

Tillie reached Main Street and turned left in the direction of

Grand. Her first stop was at Beatty & Karr's Dry Goods, at the corner of Main and Grand streets, about a 15-minute walk from Centenary. After browsing for a few minutes, she bought a large spool of cotton thread. Proprietor George Beatty, who waited on her, recalled that she was wearing kid gloves and was carrying a purse. As Beatty rang up the sale, a few minutes before 8 o'clock, she told him that she was going to attend that evening's performance by Fitzgerald's Merrymakers at Shield's Hall, and asked for directions to the entrance. The Hall was located on the third floor of the same building, and the shopkeeper stepped from behind the counter and escorted her to the stairway outside his door.[17]

Little is known about Fitzgerald's Merrymakers except that they were a troupe whose performances included individual and group singing with piano and other instrumental accompaniments, dramatic recitations, and large doses of light comedy. The most expensive ticket at Shield's Hall entitled the bearer to an individual reserved chair directly in front of the performers; holders of less expensive tickets used plain wooden benches in the rear, where Tillie was seated with two acquaintances, the sisters Mary and Agnes Wright.

When the performance ended — by most estimates, between 9:35 and 9:40 p.m.[18] — Tillie and the Wright sisters left Shield's Hall, crossed Main Street toward the front of the American House, and paused momentarily at the corner of High Street. As they waited to cross and begin walking downtown toward Church Street, another young woman overtook them — with two young men in tow. Annie Van Syckle, a 17-year-old friend of Tillie's from Waterloo and an acquaintance of the Wright sisters, had met two traveling salesmen from nearby Port Jervis, N.Y., Harry Haring and Charles Munnich.

Haring sold fancy silk handkerchiefs for a New York City company; Munnich represented his father's shoe factory. The salesmen had arrived in Hackettstown that afternoon — Haring at around 2 p.m., Munnich a couple of hours later. Each had checked into the American House and, having no other plans for the evening, decided to see the show at Shield's Hall. Neither had been aware of the other's presence in the hotel until Haring recognized Munnich's name in the hotel register as a casual acquaintance from his home town. Afterward, when Haring saw Munnich during the performance, seated a row or two behind, he identified himself.[19]

At the show, Haring had lost little time striking up a conversation with Annie Van Syckle, who was seated next to him. Afterward, as the audience began leaving, he offered to escort her home and gave her a false (and ironically appropriate) name — Hunter — as they went downstairs. Munnich, who was not far behind, saw the couple standing directly in front of him on the sidewalk as he reached the ground floor. Haring called him over and began introducing him to Annie by another false name — referring to Munnich as "Schofield"[20] — but before the introduction could be completed Annie had spotted Tillie and the Wright sisters across Main Street, and led both salesmen up behind them.

Munnich was introduced to Mary Wright by Haring as "my good friend...," with Haring pausing for a few seconds until Munnich got the point and introduced himself using the name "Schofield" that Haring had concocted for him. Other introductions and a brief round of conversation followed, and soon the entire group was strolling downtown together, two by two: Haring-alias-Hunter with Annie Van Syckle, Munnich-alias-Schofield with Mary Wright, and Tillie Smith, with 16-year-old Agnes Wright, bringing up the rear.[21]

After a few minutes they reached Trinity Methodist Church, where the Wright sisters, Tillie and Munnich stopped and regrouped. Annie Van Syckle and Harry Haring, apparently deep in conversation, continued walking downtown until they were out of sight. At that moment, three young toughs walked past the church, and one paused to mutter a few words to Mary Wright before walking on.

Mary suddenly remembered that she had promised to meet a friend, George Search, after the show.[22] Bidding Tillie Smith and Charles Munnich goodnight, she walked off with her sister. Munnich was now alone with Tillie in front of the church and offered to escort her home. She agreed, and the two crossed Main

Street — but, as they started up Church Street and were passing the post office, they heard a low whistle. The young shoe salesman became aware that two male figures were standing only a few yards away from him; while he could barely see them, Tillie seemed to recognize them. She left Munnich's side and walked over to where they stood, spoke with them for only a few seconds, then returned to her escort and continued walking with him down Church Street toward the Institute's Jefferson Street gate. They arrived there less than 10 minutes later.[23]

They stopped to talk after walking several feet inside the grounds, but within a minute or two they saw the lights being turned out all over the building and heard the snap of the front-door bolt being thrown. Munnich checked his pocket watch, noting that it was 10 minutes past 10; Tillie, who must have heard the Seminary's clock striking the hour just a few minutes before, reached over to look at the watch herself.[24] Then, after casually remarking that it was past curfew and that she would have to enter through the laundry room in the rear of the building, she picked up the thread of their conversation. Another minute or two passed, and Munnich offered to pay for a room if Tillie would return to the American House with him for the night. His proposition was declined, and she turned and walked quickly toward the Institute.

As he retraced his steps through the gate and set off at a brisk walk back up Church Street, the young "drummer" from Port Jervis heard the echo of Tillie's footsteps on the narrow boardwalk leading from the front of the building to its side and rear. He never looked back.

Several minutes later, as he neared the post office corner, he saw a gang of young rowdies across Main Street; they were lighting matches in the faces of a strolling couple to see them better.[25] He recognized the strollers as Harry Haring and Annie Van Syckle. They had apparently continued walking downtown on Main Street all the way to the Warren House, turned back uptown, and were nearing Trinity Methodist Church opposite the post office corner when they encountered the gang. No words were exchanged and, after a few seconds, they walked on.

Munnich reached the American House less than five minutes after observing the match incident, and barely 15 minutes after leaving Tillie on the Institute's walkway. As he approached the hotel's front desk, he saw salesman Isaac Baldwin standing there. Baldwin was a family friend, and the two exchanged greetings and had a brief discussion about their respective businesses.[26]

Haring, meanwhile, continued walking uptown with Annie Van Syckle, going as far as the American House before turning back toward the Washington Street home of Seward Lamson, where she worked as a domestic. His offer to her of several fancy silk handkerchiefs for sexual favors got him nothing more than a polite refusal, but when they arrived at the Lamsons' front gate and he asked if he might meet her again the following night, she assented, with a warm goodnight kiss.

The evening ended on a sour note when she had to rouse Mr. Lamson at 10:40 p.m., to re-enter the house and was scolded for keeping such late hours. Haring, who had no intention of being around the following day, left the Lamsons' doorstep and walked directly to the American House, where several guests saw him seated in the taproom with Munnich at a few minutes before 11 p.m.

As they had their nightcaps, the salesmen compared notes, each boasting to the other that he had "gotten some," with Munnich adding that he had taken Tillie under some bushes and had to pay her a dollar afterward.

Within hours, a very frightened Munnich would be swearing before a coroner's inquest that he had only engaged in a bit of harmless bragging to impress his companion.[28]

The discovery of Tillie Smith's body, as depicted in the *National Police Gazette* on May 1, 1886. In fact, the body was lying on its back.

Chapter Two

The discovery of Tillie's body the next morning at the rear of Centenary's grounds, several hundred feet from the laundry room entrance, was described as causing the greatest excitement of anything that had happened for years.[1] It was found at 8:40 a.m. by John White, who saw it lying just outside the southwestern corner of the Seminary grounds, next to a partially collapsed fence of horizontal boards.

White had been walking with his dog along the First Avenue border of the Institute grounds, headed toward Hackettstown Mayor Samuel Reese's farm a short distance beyond. First Avenue was completed for only about two-thirds of the way between Plane and Moore streets, and the decaying board fence marked its end. As White drew nearer to it, his dog began acting strangely, whining and running back and forth. White then saw a woman's body lying a short distance beyond the collapsed boards, in the direction of Moore Street.[2]

White ran the rest of the way to Reese's farm and called the mayor away from his sowing. Reese told White to go into Hackettstown at once and summon the coroner. Seeing milkman Calvin Cutler approaching in his cart, they waved him over and explained the situation, and Reese asked him to give White a ride. Before separating, the three men walked back to the end of First Avenue to examine the scene in more detail.

Their later descriptions were identical. Tillie lay on her back at an angle to the line of the fence, fully dressed, with her feet crossed and one arm outstretched. Except for finger-shaped bruises encircling her neck, and a small cut on one hand, there were no signs of violence.[3] Her cloak partially covered one arm, and her dress was carefully smoothed down, its lower hem only an inch or two above her shoe-tips; her jacket was partially on, one arm thrust through the armhole and the other out. Her gloves and purse were gone. Although her normally pinned-up hair was disheveled, hairpins were nowhere to be seen.

All agreed that the body seemed to have been carefully deposited, rather than dumped at the site.

A hemlock plank about 6 feet long lay across the victim's outstretched arm. While both Cutler and White thought it had come from the partially collapsed fence, Reese measured it and found it was 6 inches too short to fit the fence.[4]

The two men rode off in the milk cart, but since Cutler had not made his morning delivery to the Institute, he asked if he might stop there first and report the discovery before going on to the coroner's.

Titus' shift had ended at 7 a.m. and he had already gone home by the time they arrived. The day-shift janitor, Lewis Ayers, was on duty. He told the men he had just heard that one of the kitchen helpers had gone out the night before and had not been seen since. The victim was soon identified as the missing worker, and the news spread around the Institute so quickly that within minutes a crowd of more than 100 people had gathered at the scene to view the body and speculate about it.[5]

There was little evidence at that moment to substantiate it, but "(t)he theory generally accepted," according to the *Star*, "was that the girl had been brutally outraged and murdered and the body taken to (that) place."[6]

Coroner Jesse Smith arrived at the field behind the Institute at around 9:45 a.m. and he, Dr. John S. Cook and the latter's son, Dr. Richard Cook, made a preliminary examination of the victim's body where it lay.[7]

By 11:30 a.m., a coroner's jury had been empaneled at the American House.

After Smith had given permission for the body to be removed, it was taken in an ice chest to King & Bowlby, furniture manufacturers and undertakers, to await examination.

An autopsy was conducted at 2:30 that afternoon in the undertakers' upstairs workroom, with the elder Dr. Cook presiding, and with his son and several other doctors, undertaker Frank Bowlby and his assistant, William Wieder, as witnesses.[8]

Tillie's body was removed from the ice chest and placed on a smooth, wide board supported by sawhorses. Her clothing was first examined in place, and then removed and placed in a bundle on the floor to be delivered to Coroner Smith for safekeeping. She was fully dressed. Neither her outer garments nor undergarments showed signs of having been ripped, and were unremarkable except that large quantities of claylike dust and wood fibers were ground into the lower folds of the dress. Since only one of the victim's arms was in the corresponding armhole of her jacket, it appeared as if someone had tried unsuccessfully to dress the body after death. There were one or two small urine stains on the undergarments, two blood stains on the jacket collar, and one or two oily red stains, not blood, on the bottom of the dress. The outer edges of her almost-new shoes had numerous scrapes and scuffs.

The doctors next examined the exterior of the body. The hair was disheveled and the face congested, but there were no obvious traces of violence until they came to the neck — the ugly purple bruises encircling it indicated strangulation. A small cut on the left thumb had the appearance of an old reopened wound, and the only other external mark on the body was a small bruise on the upper left arm, near the shoulder.[9]

Next, Tillie's hair was cut off and thrown onto a sheet of paper on the floor, and the scalp and skull top removed for examination of the brain. No abnormalities were seen except for an effusion of dark blood just below the skin in the vicinity of both temples, apparently caused by one or more blows to each side of the head. The skin was not broken and the underlying tissues not severely damaged, suggesting that a fist had been used, rather than a club or other instrument.[10]

The examination proceeded to the chest and abdominal cavity, which were laid open with a large Y-shaped incision. The abdomen was normal, and the heart and lungs healthy, but the left lung was totally collapsed.

Dr. Cook finally came to the reproductive organs, which were removed, examined, and then returned to the abdominal cavity.

He would later testify at the inquest that, although the deceased was not pregnant and had never borne a child, she was not a virgin at the time of his examination. There was ample evidence that sexual intercourse had occurred around the time of death; in fact, the large quantity of semen recovered by the medical examiners[11] led to speculation that two or more men might have been involved. There was no evidence of forcible penetration, but Dr. Cook inferred from all the circumstances that the cause of death was strangulation committed during rape.

Judging from the condition of the body, Dr. Cook estimated that Tillie had been dead at least six or seven hours before he first examined her in the field, probably since midnight.[12]

While the coroner's jury was still assembling at the American House, Hackettstown authorities sent a telegram to the Pinkerton detective agency in New York City asking for assistance. Detective Frank, one of the agency's leading operatives, received the message and arrived in Hackettstown shortly after the inquest had opened. Within a few hours of his arrival, Frank discovered what appeared to be strong evidence that the crime had been committed a short distance from where the body was found, in a barn belonging to the Stewart family. There appeared to be signs of a recent struggle, including handprints and footprints in the dust on the floor, and stains resembling blood on a door frame. Since the body had lain almost directly in line between the barn and one of the Institute's cesspools, Frank speculated that the murderer had been carrying it there from the barn but had been frightened away before he could dispose of it.[13]

Meanwhile, the inquest had begun taking statements.

John White, Mayor Reese and Calvin Cutler testified about discovering the body, and the doctors Cook related details of their examinations.

James Titus testified that Tillie told him she planned to come in after curfew and that she threatened to stay out all night rather than go to the matron for permission.

Annie Van Syckle and the Wright sisters told of their meeting with the salesmen and of seeing Tillie go off with the one whose correct name, they now learned, was Charles Munnich.

When it was discovered that Munnich and Haring had left town on the Friday morning train, warrants were issued for their arrest. Haring was found only a few miles away in Washington,

N.J., on Friday afternoon, and was brought back to Hackettstown later that evening. Munnich, arrested in Stroudsburg, Pa., the following morning, returned to Hackettstown a few hours later on the noon train, accompanied by his father and the family's lawyer.[14]

On Saturday morning, while Munnich was being arrested in Stroudsburg, Detective Frank escorted the coroner's jury through Stewart's barn to share his discoveries with them. They had heard the Cooks testify that rape and strangulation had occurred, and they had heard evidence that Tillie was a robust and very strong young woman. Now anger and revulsion rose in the small barn as the jurymen saw for themselves what the Pinkerton investigator described as evidence of a desperate struggle.

When they returned to the American House, the coroner's jury reviewed separate written statements from Munnich and Haring, and questioned the two relentlessly about their activities during the past several days. Both salesmen admitted that they were out looking for some fun on the night of the murder, and that their intentions toward the young women were less than honorable. But Munnich swore that his statement to Haring about paying Tillie for sex was untrue, and that he had made it only because Haring had boasted of having succeeded with Annie Van Syckle.

Still, the jurors couldn't help but feel that the "drummers" were involved in some way. Munnich seemed sincere enough; but Haring, a hard-drinking, cigarette-smoking pool player, had credibility problems.

Testimony continued. Jesse Baggot testified that he was at the show at Shield's Hall with Frank Weeder who was Tillie's former boyfriend, George Search, and Aaron Hann, and they had all walked downtown together afterward. Baggot had seen Tillie, Annie and the Wright sisters while they were still in the hall, and then saw them next opposite the post office, where Weeder had called Mary Wright aside and spoken with her.

Charles Huff testified that he and three of his friends — Harold Keggan, William McWilliams and Paul Johnston — comprised the group that had held matches in Haring's face, thus placing the handkerchief salesman on Main Street some distance away from where Tillie had been last seen. Weeder admitted that he had spoken with Mary Wright at the post office corner, only to caution her about the strangers she was with, and immediately afterward had joined Hann, Search and Tineman and had gone to Tineman's store to drink cider. He added that he saw nothing more of the strangers or the women after leaving the post office corner.[15]

Munnich, meanwhile, offered to bring Isaac Baldwin back to Hackettstown to corroborate the time of his own return to the American House. The young shoe salesman's testimony was forceful, convincing and unshakable.

By Saturday night, the inquest had not yet reached a verdict. Since local elections were scheduled for Monday, a recess was declared until Tuesday morning.

On Sunday, at Detective Frank's request, Dr. Whitney asked the male students to turn out and scour the Seminary grounds in search of Tillie's gloves, purse and hairpins. Their only discovery was a half-empty liquor bottle near the spot where the body had been found.[16]

At this point, the Pinkerton detective joined state Detective John F. McClallen in pursuing another lead. Two tramps had been seen on a street near the Seminary on Thursday evening; two tramps, one of whom had a scratched face, had also been seen around the Hackettstown railroad depot early Friday morning. Two men answering their general descriptions, David Sleight and George Brown, were arrested at the Delaware Water Gap on Sunday and taken to Stroudsburg. They were a thoroughly disreputable pair, rough and uncouth, and Sleight had a prison record. When the two refused to return to New Jersey voluntarily, McClallen and Frank took the Sunday night train to Stroudsburg and interviewed them at 8 o'clock the following morning.

Their account of their whereabouts on the night of the murder was checked and found to be untrue. While they claimed to have spent that night in Belvidere at a certain Joseph Fisher's, Fisher said he hadn't seen them for months. Sleight had a fresh scratch on his face, which he said he had gotten in an accident.[17]

The detectives, encouraged by this, obtained an extradition order and were ready to serve it, when the suspects changed their minds and agreed to come to New Jersey. A large crowd assembled to meet Sleight and Brown on their arrival in Hackettstown on Wednesday evening, and followed them from the depot to the American House. Their guards spirited them through the hotel doors and into the inquest's meeting room.

Hopes for a speedy solution to the case were dashed, though. The pair simply admitted that they had lied about where they had spent Thursday night. They gave the name of another individual in whose barn they had slept, and this time the alibi was verified. As for the scratch on Sleight's face, his claim that he had gotten it when he tripped over a pile of wood in a lumber yard was substantiated by friends and relatives. The reason for the tramps' lying to the investigators remained a mystery and the authorities, while angry, took no punitive action.[18]

Now, Munnich's and Haring's statements were corroborated by patrons of the American House, who had seen the two looking totally unruffled as they sat in the hotel taproom at 11 p.m. on April 8. It seemed unreasonable to suggest that Munnich could have committed the crime, disposed of the body and returned to the American House without a trace of excitement or disarray.

A week later, his story would receive further, unexpected corroboration from Arturo Rivera and Harry Smith, occupants of a dormitory bedroom just under the mansard roof at the front of the Seminary's north wing. From his vantage at a high windowsill, where he crouched sneaking a cigarette after lights-out, Rivera had seen a man and a woman coming through the gate a little after the lights-out bell had rung on the night of April 8. Rivera called his roommate to the window, and both observed the couple as they walked several feet inside the grounds, stopped and spoke, and then separated. They saw the man walk back into Church Street, while the woman disappeared from their view as she neared the front of the building. It was not until they returned from spring vacation and learned of Munnich's testimony that they realized the significance of what they had seen and came forward as witnesses in his behalf.[19]

$25

&*Use Ink, and write plainly, especially names.

1. Full name of deceased *Matilda Smith*
(If an infant not named, so state, and give sex.)

2. Age *18* years .... months .... days .... hours.

3. Color *White* ... Occupation *Domestic*

4. Single, ~~married, widow or widower~~ ...... { Cross out all but } the right one. }

5. Birthplace *Sussex Co. N.J.*
(State or county. If of foreign birth, give how long in the United States.)

6. Last place of residence *Hackettstown*
(If a city, give name; if not, give county and township.)
Warren Co. N.J.

7. How long resident in this State *Life*

8. Place of death *Hackettstown*
(If in a city, give name, and street and number; if in township, give name
Warren Co. N.J.
and county; if in an institution, so state.)

9. Father's name *Nathan Smith*

Country of birth *U.S.*

10. Mother's name *Sarah Smith*

Country of birth *U.S.*

11. I hereby certify that ~~I attended the deceased during the
last illness, and that~~ *she* died on the *9th*
day of *April* 1886; and that the cause of death
was *Strangulation By Some person
or persons unknown*

Length of sickness .... { See over and add } particulars. }

Jesse G. Smith
Coroner ~~Medical Attendant~~

Residence ....

Name of Undertaker *Kings Reily*

Residence of Undertaker *Hackettstown N.J.*

Place of Burial *Hackettstown*

Tillie Smith's death certificate, signed by Coroner Jesse Smith. Note that the official date of death is April 9.

As for Haring, it was grudgingly acknowledged that he had even less opportunity to commit the crime. He had been placed with certainty on Main Street at about 10:20 p.m. by Charles Huff, at the Lamsons' on Washington Street at about 10:40 p.m., and back at the American House no more than 15 minutes afterward.

While the inquest deliberated, King & Bowlby made preparations for Tillie's burial. Her hair, which had been removed during the autopsy, was combed out and rearranged on her head, and she was dressed in a long white dress, with a high collar to hide the bruises around her neck. The undertakers remained open all day Sunday and Monday to accommodate those who came to pay their respects — including the victim's mother, who threw herself on the coffin and cried out for vengeance against her daughter's murderers.

On Tuesday, April 13, the body was removed to a receiving vault at Union Cemetery while arrangements were made for burial the following day. Since Tillie's family was unable to pay for her funeral, all the expenses were assumed by the town, and Union Cemetery donated a modest plot in an area reserved for the indigent.[20]

There was no clergyman on hand to eulogize Tillie on Wednesday morning, and her simple coffin was lowered into the earth quickly and unceremoniously. Then, as the mourners were starting to leave and the gravediggers were reaching for their shovels, Dr. Whitney arrived in great haste and asked everyone to remain while he read the service. Although scheduled to officiate, he had been summoned the same morning to testify at the inquest and had been unable to make other arrangements. His eulogy dwelt at great length on chastity, strength of character, and the virtuous and blameless life of the young victim who had preferred death to dishonor.[21] When he finished, the gravediggers resumed their work, and clods of earth thumped hollowly on the coffin as the grave was filled in.

The day ended on a disappointing note. At a few minutes before midnight, the coroner's jury decided it had done all it could to determine the circumstances surrounding Tillie's death, and rendered a verdict that the victim:

> between the hours of 10:15 p.m. on April 8, 1886, and 8:45 a.m. on April 9, 1886, at Hackettstown…was by some person or persons to the jurors at present unknown, with force and arms feloniously killed in an attempt at rape, that her death was caused by strangulation, and appearances indicate that the assault took place in the vacant barn on the Margaret Stewart property to the rear of the Seminary grounds.[22]

Coroner Smith issued a death certificate. With all leads gone, Detective Frank left the case, saying Tillie's murder would probably join the ranks of unsolved crimes. Munnich and Haring were released on $500 bond each as material witnesses. Brown and Sleight were given railroad fares and told to get out of town.

Detective Frank may have written off the murder, but members of the New York daily press had been covering it for an entire week and were not about to give up good human-interest copy so easily. During the following days their columns became sharply critical of what they presented as the authorities' ineptitude. The daily New York newspapers enjoyed wide readership in northern New Jersey, and their daily criticism of local competence soon became an embarrassment. In response to mounting pressure, a number of prominent citizens petitioned the Mayor and Common Council on April 19 to authorize a $1,000 reward for information leading to the arrest and conviction of the person or persons responsible.

Their petition read, in part:

> We are the more earnest in making this request because of the horrible nature of the crime and because the hitherto good name of our community is sadly injured, and because the daily press and other communities are widely censuring our town because we have not yet offered any reward for the detection of the guilty.[23]

The reward was approved by the end of the day. Dr. Whitney was author of the petition. It seems clear that the pillars of the community were beginning to work at correcting the impression that Hackettstown cared little about crime victims unless they were from the proper class — the kind of theme played repeatedly and with consummate skill by *The World* in that time of social and labor unrest.

Meanwhile, assurance that the investigation would not flag was provided by *The Tribune, The Sun, The Herald* and, of course, *The World*, all of which sent reporters to Hackettstown to cover its progress. *The World's* articles are used throughout this narrative because they provide the most egregious examples of the 19th century New York journalistic style. It should be added that James Creelman covered the case for *The World*, and that "yellow journalism" is believed to have made its first appearance in his coverage.[24]

The first of Creelman's columns questioning the handling of the case appeared on April 21 under the heading: "Tillie Smith's Murderer — Citizens of Hackettstown Do Not Believe That She Was Killed by Tramps." It opened by reporting the council's posting of a reward. After noting that "since Frank, the Pinkerton detective, left the case very little (was) done apparently in the way of detective work," the reporter went on to play detective himself, asserting that "very few people believe in the theory that Tillie Smith was murdered in Mrs. Stewart's red barn." It continued:

> The victim was a pure, mild-mannered young girl, born and reared in her father's farmhouse in Sussex County. She was employed as a potato-peeler in the kitchen of the big Methodist Institute here. Never, save on the night of the murder, was she known to stay out after the doors were locked, at 10 o'clock at night. She had been to an entertainment in the main street and returned in company with Charles Munnich, the Port Jervis shoe drummer whose acquaintance she made that night. The pair was seen to walk towards the Institute. One witness says that it was at 10:30 o'clock. Munnich swore before the coroner's jury that when he left the girl at the front gate of the seminary she looked at her watch and said it was 10:10. The young man was seen in the American Hotel, where he stopped, in the neighborhood of 11 o'clock. It is scarcely probable that he would have assaulted and murdered the girl and have dragged her body to where it was found in that short time. Much less likely is it that he could have induced an innocent girl to climb a fence or make a long detour on a dark night in order to get into a vacant barn. The presence of

the girl in this barn is hardly likely in any case. It would be hard to convince an ordinary man that anybody could wheedle a virtuous maid into such a place. The motive would have been quite apparent to her, and the fact that she apparently defended her honor with all her strength refutes the idea that she assented to improper proposals. All those who saw the body of Tillie as it lay carefully arranged and disposed in the rear of the Institute grounds seem to believe that the girl was murdered close to the Institute building and was carried, not dragged, to where her body was found. The authorities of the Institute seem anxious to avoid the necessary inference. Dr. Whitney, the respected President of the establishment, has expressed his conviction that it was a mistake to release Munnich and his companion Haring, who was with him on the night of the murder. The theory that tramps committed the crime is believed by no one here — in fact, the whole town considerably inclines to the belief that Hackettstown still contains the murderer. The next few days may furnish some light.[25]

This short article is significant for its wealth of inconsistencies, speculations and outright inaccuracies.

Those who first saw the body as it lay in the field did not believe that the murder was committed close to the Institute building, but rather in the Stewart barn, as the coroner's jury afterward determined officially.

Munnich was exculpated because he could not have dragged the body, yet a few sentences later the writer states that the murderer carried the body to the spot where it was found.

Tillie Smith might never have stayed out beyond 10 p.m. after she began working at the Institute, but Dr. Conover had talked about her returning home late when she worked for him. She was also known to have gone out at night with Frank Weeder several times and to have been denied permission by the matron to return after curfew on the one occasion on which she had requested it.

The autopsy was inconclusive as to Tillie's prior condition of virginity.

Opinion was divided about whether she was timid or brave; here, again, Dr. Conover was surely of the latter opinion, yet the reporter described her as "mild-mannered."

Had Tillie defended herself "with all her strength?" Her body displayed few if any signs of a struggle and her clothing was undamaged, although *The World* inaccurately reported on April 10 that there was a "large ugly bruise" on her forehead and that her clothing "hung in shreds about her body."

And Tillie did not own a watch. Munnich had testified that she had looked at his watch after he announced that it was 10:10 p.m.

The local newspapers, although more closely in touch with the climate of opinion in the community and urging moderation upon their readers, seemed powerless against the onslaught of big-city journalism. All of them published weekly, while *The World* and its New York competitors had the advantage of hammering away at the case daily. If the newspapers' production timing is taken into account, no local newspaper on or about April 22 had yet reported that Hackettstown's authorities were focusing the investigation on any individual.

On that day, however, *The World* first spoke definitively about the "one man in this town who knew that the girl was likely to be on the Institute grounds after the door was locked..."[26]

The same day's *Star* reported that:

(T)he numerous theories advanced show the diversity of opinion on the subject. Some think that, although the Coroner's jury cleared them, Munnich and Haring are in some unaccountable manner connected with the mystery. Others think that the girl ventured to sleep in the barn, and the same proved to be occupied by tramps, who alone are responsible and guilty. Institute boys are suspected by others, and town boys by many. The numerous discussions by the different theorists are spirited and not void of strong points of argument on every side. The fact is, there is about as much ground for belief in one as in the others.[27]

The *Republican* focused on the growing suspicion that Stewart's barn was not the murder site, apparently lapsing into exaggeration as it scrambled to join the metropolitan journals' camp:

It is now an almost universally accepted theory that the murder occurred on the Institute grounds, and that the body was never farther away from the Institute than where it lay when discovered. This does away entirely with the barn theory, which seems a surprisingly absurd one, and it is strange that it was generally accepted in the beginning.[28]

The *Belvidere Apollo's* more accurate account appeared on the same day:

(t)he idea that the guilt lies somewhere about the Institute is started and encouraged, although there is no evidence circumstantial or other — to advance the idea.[29]

One day later, *The World* had progressed from vague references to the "one man in this town," to pointing the finger of suspicion at James Titus without actually naming him.

Under the sub-heading "What Janitor Titus Says About His Movements on the Night of the Crime," *The World* said:

Common sense points strongly to one man who is in the town. Men whisper and wink, but they do not name him aloud. The man bears a good reputation; is a hard-working, faithful employee; a constant husband, and, so far as can be ascertained, a man of good habits. Today he is pale, nervous and almost haggard, because he knows that he is suspected. His actions and appearance would be very natural in an innocent man of a sensitive disposition. Go where you will in Hackettstown, examine any clue, reason out any theory, and at the end of them all this man looms up.[30]

The story included still more speculation about the crime. Much was made of the missing hairpins, gloves and purse, and it was conjectured that, since they hadn't been found, the murderer must have disposed of them. If the murderer had disposed of them, he must have been able to gather them up. If he gathered them up, he must have had privacy and light in which to work, so the murder must have been committed indoors.

The conclusion: Only a person who was in the Institute could have had proper privacy and light to pick up the hairpins.

The weakness of this conclusion should have been obvious: The Institute was not the only place in the area in which there might have been both privacy and light, but no one seemed to care.

More followed: Since Tillie's gloves, purse and breast pin had not been found near her body, the murderer must have destroyed them, along with the hairpins, to protect himself. Wasn't there a furnace in the Institute basement?

No one seems to have considered robbery as an explanation, or the near-impossibility of finding a handful of hairpins that might be lying somewhere on the 10-acre campus.

Once the speculative ball began rolling there was no stopping it.

A red stain found at the bottom of Tillie's dress was assumed to be red lead, a substance used in pipe-fitting, because plumbing work was often done in the Institute basement and there were traces of red lead on the floor.

The minute hemlock fibers in the back of Tillie's dress were, likewise, assumed to come from the basement because carpentry was done there and some sawdust was on the floor.

The singular term "murderer" began to be used, although the autopsy evidence suggested that more than one person could have been involved in the crime.

The following day's edition of *The World* finally referred to Titus by name in the body of its article about the Hackettstown murder. Under the heading "A Web of Circumstantial Evidence Slowly Being Woven Around the Suspected Man by the Detectives," it stated:

> The name of one man is on everybody's lips, and why he has not been arrested is a mystery. There is no direct evidence against him, but the circumstances of the case, stripped of all strained theories and looked at in a natural way, form a terrible chain around him. Janitor Titus still makes his daily rounds at the Institute. He is apparently wasting away, and all the color has left his face. Today he said he knew he was under suspicion. If the girl was strangled in the cellar-like drying room of that dark basement, to which the side door of the rear entrance led, the murderer would probably have got rid of the body. The breast-pin, hair-pins, purse, spool of thread and gloves would, in all probability, have been scattered on the floor during the struggle. When the murderer returned it would have been a common-sense precaution for him to

gather up all these things and fling them into the furnace. The girl entered at the front gate. Titus knew she wanted to be admitted by the side door, and he alone could have answered her rap.[31]

On April 25, under the heading "Was It By The Furnace?":

If the man whom the majority of Hackettstown people suspect of the murder of Tillie Smith is guilty his anguish must be something beyond description. He is tied to the spot where the poor girl was strangled and assaulted, for to leave it would be to confess his guilt.

Given the ferocity of these daily attacks, public belief in the likelihood of Titus' guilt began to take hold. Once that happened, even the janitor's most casual remarks would be interpreted as strengthening the case against him.

This same April 25 column attempted to debunk another theory of the rape-murder that had begun to circulate: that young members of a town gang, Frank Weeder among them, were responsible.

Weeder, described as having formerly been "the accepted beau and escort of Tillie on the four or five occasions when she went out at night," reportedly said that he, with a friend, had whistled to Tillie that night when she and Munnich had just entered Church Street. The column went on to state that Weeder also admitted to being among the young toughs who had held matches up to the faces of Harry Haring and Annie Van Syckle as they walked on Main Street that night.

Interestingly, any theory of Weeder's involvement was dismissed out-of-hand: He wasn't a suitable subject of suspicion because he was not particularly intelligent, while "the surroundings and apparent method of the crime and the concealment of all traces of it show great intelligence."

Weeder was described as speaking "frankly and without nervousness" as he described himself and his relationship with Tillie Smith:

"I know I have been reckless and rather tough around the town, but I don't think anybody ought to suspect me of such a horrible crime as this because of my folly. I was well acquainted with

Tillie and was for a short time her beau. She was a modest, quiet girl, and, in my opinion, knew how to take care of herself thoroughly. I have always acted in a gentlemanly way with her and she never gave me any reason to believe that she would tolerate any other conduct. I have kissed her goodnight several times, but I never even put my arm around her waist. I don't believe she would have allowed any man to do so. Tillie was not the kind of girl who would have been persuaded to go to a barn or to the rear fields after the doors of the Institute were locked and the lights were out. I was told that she once arose in the Institute church to be prayed for. She was certainly a very moral girl."[32]

The reporter may have introduced this bit of information to bolster his own murder theory by discrediting others that disagreed with it, but Weeder's remarks, if true, would have been solid gold to any investigator who had done his homework. It is regrettable that *The World's* "clearance" of Weeder was repeated by state investigators, who dropped him as a suspect.

This appears to have been more than a coincidence. City reporters were deeply involved in the investigation, apparently enjoying collegial relations with the officials. Was *The World's* assessment of Weeder, superficial as it might have been, given as much weight by the investigators as a report made by one of their own? This could explain their subsequent failure to pursue what would have been a promising line of investigation, about which more will be said later.

As for James Titus, who can doubt that by this time he was pale and drawn? His haggard appearance, no doubt due as much to ill health as to the strain of realizing he was emerging as the suspect in a capital murder case, was now pointed out as evidence of a guilty conscience.

The World's attacks continued. On April 26, its reporter opened with: "The murderer of Tillie Smith is still a free man," and went on to say that "(t)he arrest of Janitor Titus is looked for hourly."

There were other insinuations in the daily articles. The authorities were supposedly dragging their feet because of Titus' position in the community; the case was an embarrassment to the

Methodist establishment, which was trying to have it swept under the rug; that it might go down as just another unsolved crime unless something was done immediately.

The message to Hackettstown was clear: There would be no respite until they had named the suspect and made an arrest.

During the last week of April, there began a movement in Hackettstown to erect a monument to Tillie Smith. A closer look at the activity discloses that its earliest mention in a local newspaper was on April 29, when it was reported that Mayor Reese had published an appeal.

The following week's edition of the *Warren Republican* indicates that the first call for contributions went out on Tuesday, April 27,[34] yet *The World* of April 28 reported that the first contributions for that purpose had been received by Mayor Reese on the 27th and the subscription books issued late that same day. The *Warren Republican* reported that, during the first week in May, a committee of Hackettstown citizens, including Mayor Reese, Dr. Whitney and the superintendent of Union Cemetery, met in its offices "for the purpose of taking action as to the collection, management and disposition of the monument fund."[35]

Both timing and the wording indicate that a drive was already well under way when the Hackettstown group met for the first time. Perhaps damage control was also on that evening's agenda. A recent letter to the editor of *The World* had complained about "the almost shameful act of permitting the burial of (Tillie's) body in a pauper's grave,"[36] and with that same newspaper making reference to "the hundreds of letters received daily" containing money for a monument, the town leaders must surely have felt hard-pressed to do something quickly.

The World had published a drawing of an "unsolicited" monument design, actually a plaster model 3 feet high, supposedly received anonymously at the newspaper's Manhattan offices.

The design was just bad enough to have a ring of authenticity about it. So, too, did the anonymous sculptor's accompanying letter:

"Reading in the papers about the heroism of Tillie Smith, I became enthusiastic and modelled [sic] this new and beautiful sub-

36

ject as a design for the proposed monument, and have succeeded in getting a quite original composition. My friends who have seen this model were delighted, and advised me to send it to THE WORLD, which no doubt will see that it will be executed in heroic size and in pure white marble. My friends believe that by selling miniature copies the fund would grow rapidly. The cross is proposed to be cast in iron, gilded, and of a sufficient height to be seen from a distance. I represent the heroine struggling with the reptile, holding firmly with her right hand the myrtle crown which symbolizes chastity. Her path is strewn with thorns."[37]

The drawing reappeared in the *Republican* on May 14. It is remarkable that this first tangible expression of a monument was delivered to *The World's* offices in finished form within days of that newspaper's first mentioning anything about a monument. One might speculate not only whether the design was in the works for a somewhat longer time, but whether it was calculated to shift the public focus toward obtaining something better, and away from the question of whether anything so elaborate was needed at all.

On the day of Titus' arrest, the balance in the monument fund contained $146.[38] Two weeks later, it had risen to nearly $450. Meanwhile, the Monument Committee had estimated that the memorial depicted in *The World* would cost about $2,000 to execute, and its members were reluctant to contract with a monument-maker until they had a better idea of how much they could raise.[39]

In the interim, the trustees of Union Cemetery agreed to donate their best plot so that whichever memorial was selected would eventually be erected there.

Dr. Whitney, ever sensitive to the Institute's public relations needs, had previously made a statement to the press in which he expressed regret "that the body of the dead girl was ever consigned to a pauper's grave."

He added: "But this was permitted during the great excitement *and before the true significance of her death had dawned upon us.*"[emphasis added][40]

Meanwhile, the Monument Committee's subscription books

The first monument design submitted to *The World* in May 1886.

for a memorial to the heroic struggle of "the poor little country girl"[41] were circulating far and wide.

Was the monument program another of Joseph Pulitzer's circulation-boosting schemes? A master at plucking at the public heart strings for gain, Pulitzer was the driving force behind the previous year's subscription to raise funds for the Statue of Liberty's pedestal. His hand seems evident in the declaration, supposedly written by Mayor Reese, that appeared on the front page of each:

> Desiring to attest our appreciation of the character of the noble girl, Matilda Smith, who gave her life to the cause of virtue and honor on the night of April 8, 1886, we whose names are herewith appended, do hereby pledge ourselves in the sums subscribed toward the purchase of a suitable tombstone or monument over the spot where now rest her remains — in the Union Cemetery at Hackettstown — or at some other place in the Town hereafter to be determined upon. All who think a pure life, even though it be a humble one, and a noble death in the cause of virtue and true womanhood is worth commemorating are requested to subscribe.[42]

The effect of the campaign was like touching a match to tinder. Tillie's fierce but futile struggle in defense of her honor became an undeniable truth and a cause célèbre that took on a life of its own. A column in the *Hackettstown Gazette*, titled "A Monument to Virtue," supported the movement "to commemorate virtue and chastity, in the defense of which (Tillie) lost her life."

It continued:

> Tillie Smith, born and reared among surroundings that were anything but moral and elevating, when put to the test by the lustful villain who choked her to death on that fatal Thursday night, chose death to dishonor. She had naught in this world but that precious jewel — virtue, and of that she would not be despoiled. Her gallant struggle and horrible death in defense of her all should be fittingly commemorated. By all means let a substantial monument be erected over brave Tillie Smith, that for generations shall stand as a symbol of the world's appreciation of a virtuous woman.[43]

A list of subscribers' names was printed, and with it some

of the letters that accompanied contributions by New Yorkers and reflected prevailing sentiment. One, containing a donation of one dollar in the name of a female student at Centenary, read:

> The lesson she taught at the cost of her life is one which hundreds of even gentle bred cultivated girls may learn, and when they look upon the pure white marble may realize the value of purity and fight for it even though they lay down their life in defense.

And another, containing a contribution of 25 cents:

> Please overlook the small amount for I am poor, but would nevertheless like to do all I can to help a cause which will help us to remember a virtuous girl struggling against a brute.

In this same column, mention was first made of relocating Tillie's grave. On Saturday, May 22, only six weeks after the murder, the Monument Committee staked off Union Cemetery's best plot, H-55 on the north side of Crest Drive, the one which had been donated by the cemetery association's trustees during the committee's formative meeting.

Three days later. Tillie was exhumed from her pauper's grave. Following a brief graveside examination in which further evidence was removed from her coffin,[44] she was reburied in her prestigious new location.

There she would await the "pure white marble" that would invest her death with far greater significance than might ever have been expected of her life.

Chapter Three

James Titus was arrested at his Sharp Street home shortly after midnight on April 29 and charged with murdering Tillie Smith while attempting to rape her. Prosecutor Sylvester Smith, State Detective John P. McClallen and a third detective named Simons had arrived in Hackettstown at various times earlier in the day, and even avoided being seen together in order not to arouse suspicion. After a brief meeting at the American House they placed their accumulated evidence before a local Justice of the Peace, Lewis J. Youngblood, who issued an arrest warrant. In deference to Titus' widowed mother, who lived with the janitor and his family, McClallen and Simons waited until after midnight before placing him under arrest, to avoid a crowd's gathering at the scene.

Titus was apparently expecting to be arrested at any moment, because his cousin, attorney George Titus, was present at the house and demanded an immediate hearing before a magistrate. By 1 a.m., a large group had crowded into Justice Youngblood's front parlor: Prosecutor Smith; Detectives McClallen and Simons; James Titus and two cousins, attorney George and state Assemblyman Thomas Titus; and two of the ubiquitous members of the press — one of whom was from *The World.*

Youngblood, roused from a sound sleep, sat there bleary-eyed in his bathrobe, a scarf wrapped around his neck. Attorney George demanded that the evidence on which his cousin's arrest was based be produced, and a hearing held then and there. The prosecutor protested that the state was not prepared to go into a hearing for several days, because witnesses had to be brought from New York. In retrospect, this seems a rather lame excuse, as the only important witnesses from New York were Haring and Munnich, who could have been brought from Port Jervis in a matter of hours.

Continuing his argument, Smith reminded Youngblood that

41

the grand jury would meet in Belvidere, the county seat, on the following Wednesday, and if the prisoner was indicted at that time he could be committed without a hearing, so it really didn't matter if he had one at the moment. There was a brief pause, followed by a hurried conference between George Titus and Prosecutor Smith. Following this, acting on his cousin's advice, the prisoner waived his right to a full hearing, and an agreement was made for his immediate commitment to jail.

The meeting was completed in a few more minutes, and the group trudged back to Sharp Street to allow Titus some rest before the planned 4 a.m. departure for Belvidere. The prisoner slept fitfully and, following a tearful farewell to his wife and mother, he entered a carriage, Bible in hand, and sat between yet another relative, B.B. Cook, and Detective McClallen. The sun had risen by the time the somber trio reached the Warren County Courthouse and the prisoner had been safely lodged in the old jail.[1]

Titus may have been behind bars, but press interest in him was still high and the prosecutors made every effort to use it to their advantage even while admitting that their case was entirely circumstantial. *The World* of April 29 first made mention of a William Meade [sic], a theological student who was Titus' occasional assistant, and who was said to have sworn to facts which fastened the crime on the janitor. One of two students who assisted the janitor, Peter F. Mead, became the state's chief witness both before the grand jury in May and the trial jury in October.

As media coverage continued, not even the normally sedate *New York Times* seemed immune from sniping at the prisoner. Its edition of April 30 reported the following rumor:

> Those in charge of the case claim that many things tending to show the prisoner's bad conduct with the female help at the institute have been voluntarily told them. Tonight Mayor Reese received a letter from a gentleman in New Brunswick saying that there was a young lady living in that city who was formerly employed at the institute, and who tells a shocking story of Titus' conduct toward her while she was here. The letter will be forwarded to the prosecutor.[2]

There was no such letter. It was never entered in evidence, or even produced, and there were no further references either by the prosecutors or *The Times* to the "many things" which it allegedly disclosed about the prisoner's behavior on the job. Yet neither the prosecutors who supposedly possessed it nor the newspaper that disclosed it was ever challenged, and no retraction was ever published.

Other, more subtle techniques were employed by the daily journals, both to convey an unfavorable image of Titus and to play on class animosities. Photographs of the prisoner and Tillie Smith were obtained by *The World*, and recreated as line drawings for the front page. Tillie emerged from the artist's pen a slim, full-bosomed young woman, with a meek expression on her face. Titus, by contrast, was transformed into a caricature of a Victorian villain. His thick handlebar mustache was thinned out, its ends made to descend almost to his chin, and his cravat was redrawn as a foppish bow.[3] The effect of juxtaposing the two was to portray young innocence seduced and destroyed by a jaded libertine.

Between 50 and 60 witnesses testified before the grand jury for three days. Annie Van Syckle and the Wright sisters were questioned, as were Harry Haring and Charles Munnich, who came back from Port Jervis for the occasion.

But the star of the show was Peter Mead. One of two students at the seminary employed as part-time helpers for the janitors, Mead worked in exchange for partial tuition and fees — usually by wheeling coal from the coal cellar to the furnace area as needed.

Both Mead and his fellow worker, a Danish exchange student named Niels Madsen, usually brought their books with them to the basement so they could study during slack periods, although Mead seems to have spent as much time talking with Titus as preparing his lessons. At 25, he was older than the other students and closer in age to Titus than to his peers.

Mead had worked as a farm manager for several years before deciding to continue his education for the ministry. Farm management undoubtedly had unpleasant associations for the janitor, whose father had committed suicide when his crops failed,

Tillie Smith and James Titus portrayed realistically in the *National Police Gazette*, October 16, 1886

Tillie Smith and James Titus depicted in *The World* on May 2, 1886. Note the difference: Titus has the addition of a leering smile, the down-turned moustache and the floppy bow tie, and Tillie appears meeker, slimmer and shapelier.

but it is likely that the men's shared conversations about the hard-ships and uncertainties of agriculture helped them develop a pleasantly informal relationship on the job. From what is known of their personalities, though, it is hard to imagine that they ever developed a close friendship. Mead tended to be pompous and a little stuffy, styling himself "Reverend" although still only a sem-inarian. Titus, on the other hand, married and a father, seems to have had a somewhat worldly sense of humor lurking beneath his taciturn exterior. He was given to playing pranks with the students on April Fool's Day, and was said to have a dry wit.[4]

Beginning in April, the seminary's steam heat system was shut down and only the hot water apparatus needed attention, so the janitor and the seminarian had even more time than usual for conversation. It was during these exchanges, Mead alleged, that Titus made his most incriminating remarks, statements indicating both his lustful intentions toward the victim before the crime and his guilty state of mind afterward.[5]

Curiously, Mead began keeping detailed notes of these con-versations almost immediately after the Hackettstown council posted the reward, but was unable to give any reason for doing it. When defense counsel later suggested that he was motivated by the thousand dollars to take advantage of his friendship with Ti-tus, he vigorously denied any such intention but provided no al-ternative explanation.[6]

The local press generally regarded the state's case as far less compelling than did the New York dailies. The Hackettstown and Washington newspapers, in particular, were quick to point out that the sheer number of witnesses summoned to testify before the grand jury indicated a case even more circumstantial than they had originally thought. The *Hackettstown Gazette* had al-ready cautioned its readers:

> It is true the air is full of theories and suspicions, and the re-porters of the metropolitan papers have woven an ingenious net-work of circumstantial evidence around James Titus and have manufactured public opinion so fast that the belief has settled into a positive conviction in the minds of a majority of our citizens that the right man has been found.

The newspaper reminded its readers that Titus deserved the presumption of innocence, saying he was "hemmed in with an almost impenetrable web of circumstantial evidence," and adding:

[N]ot one word of real evidence has been adduced to convict him of this crime...we think it would be just as well to hold off condemnation of this man until something is shown connecting him directly with [it].[7]

While the state did not dispute this characterization of its case, a detective who worked on it remarked to the reporters that in his opinion it was the clearest and strongest case of circumstantial evidence he had ever seen. After three days of testimony and deliberation, the grand jury, on Friday, May 7, returned an indictment whose counts read as follows:

...that James J. Titus, of the Town of Hackettstown, in the said County of Warren, on the 8th day of April, in the year of our Lord 1886, at the town aforesaid, and within the jurisdiction of this Court, in and upon one Matilda Smith, then and there feloniously, willfully and of his malice aforethought, did kill and murder, contrary to the form of the statute in such case made and provided, and against the peace of this State, the government and dignity of the same;

...that the said James J. Titus, on the said 8th day of April, in the year aforesaid, in said county and within the jurisdiction aforesaid, in and upon one Matilda Smith, in the peace of God and this State then and there being, did commit rape, and in attempting to commit rape, and in committing rape in and upon her, the said Matilda Smith, did kill the said Matilda Smith contrary to the form of the statute in such case made and provided, against the peace of this State the government and dignity of the same;

...that the said James J. Titus, on the eighth day of April, in the year of our Lord one thousand eight hundred and eighty-six, at the town and county aforesaid, and within the jurisdiction of this Court, with force and arms in and upon the said Matilda Smith, in the peace of God and of this State then and there being, feloniously, willfully and of his malice aforethought did make an assault, and that he, the said James J. Titus, on and about the neck and throat of the said Matilda Smith did then and there feloniously, willfully and of his malice aforethought fix, fasten and grasp with his hands, and that the said James J. Titus with his hands aforesaid, her the said Matilda Smith then and there feloniously, willfully and of his malice aforethought, did choke, suffocate and strangle, of which said choking, suffocating and strangling she, the said Matilda Smith, then and there instantly died; and so the Inquest aforesaid, on their oaths aforesaid, do say that the said James J. Titus, in manner and form aforesaid, feloniously, willfully and of his malice aforethought, her the said Matilda Smith, did kill and murder contrary to the statute in such case made and provided and against the peace of this State, the government and dignity of the same.[8]

The last count was a catch-all in the event the two dealing with rape failed — the common law crime of premeditated murder. All three counts were capital offenses, and Titus, by then, had the presence of mind to dismiss his cousin George and retain two of Warren County's most prominent attorneys, the father and son team of Jehiel G. and George M. Shipman.

On Saturday, May 8, J.G. Shipman, senior member of the firm, stood with his client before Chief Justice Mercer Beasley and associate Justices Beatty and Canfield as each count of the indictment was read. Titus was self-assured, his voice distinct and audible throughout the courtroom, as he replied to each charge: "Not guilty!"[9]

Shipman then addressed the court. His client had been poorly advised about not seeking a hearing at the time of his arrest, and since the accused was not represented before the grand jury the defense had no way of evaluating the validity of the state's charges. He asked the court to direct that the testimony taken before the coroner's jury, the affidavits of Detective McClallen and Mead, and the list of grand jury witnesses all be filed with the county clerk within 10 days. Prosecutor Smith did not object to any of the filings except Mead's affidavit, arguing that this information was for the state's sole and exclusive use, and that Titus had been taken into custody not on the strength of Mead's testimony but on the strength of Detective McClallen's alone. The court sustained Smith's objection on his assurance that Mead's statements were not taken into account in making the arrest.[10]

The prisoner, having entered his plea, was remanded to the county jail to await trial.

Later that day, the balance in the monument fund reached $885.

Prosecutor Smith appears to have been less than truthful with the Shipmans and the Court about the value of Mead's affidavit. Although the records of the grand jury are not extant, the transcript of *State v. James J. Titus* contains Mead's entire testimony. As he was the state's key witness, there is no reason to believe that his testimony before the grand jury differed substantially from that which he gave five months later at trial; indeed, major discrepancies would have resulted in his impeachment by the defense.

What would Mead's grand jury testimony have been? He would have sworn that Titus, several days before the murder, remarked to him that he thought Tillie Smith was "the kind of girl one could have a racket with if he wanted," (meaning, in the slang of the period, that he thought she was sexually available). He would have sworn that just before 8 o'clock on the night of the murder he and Titus were in the basement waiting for the plumber, and that he had told Titus he was going upstairs to study his history lesson, but the janitor had replied that he should wait around — that Titus had told him to wait because "Tillie Smith is coming in late, she'll be alone, and then we can pump her."

He would have recalled for the grand jury his startled reply: "Oh, pshaw!" and his reply that he might come down later but how, once he had returned to his room, he had studied until shortly before lights-out and was asleep by 10.

He would have related how Titus had asked him what he should say before the coroner's jury, that he had asked whether God could forgive someone who had committed such a crime as Tillie's murder, that he had hoped Mead would provide an alibi for him.

He would have testified that Titus, having been observed reading his Bible one night, remarked that the psalms were a source of comfort when one was in trouble.

He would have told how he had seen the janitor looking into

the windows of certain basement rooms from outside, as if to assess what might be observable through them, and that the man had remarked "they can hang my body, but they can never hang my soul."

While each incident Mead related would not have been fatal in and of itself, the entire string of incidents, combined with the conjectured opportunities for Titus to commit the crime and destroy the evidence, would obviously have tipped the scales in favor of indictment.

Thus, the conclusion is inescapable: Prosecutor Smith was far from truthful in discounting the value of Mead's testimony. On the contrary, he and McClallen could never have obtained an indictment without it.[11]

Spring became summer, and the defense attorneys were hard at work preparing for the opening session of the Court of Oyer and Terminer on September 28.

The Shipmans, father and son, were noted for their courtroom eloquence and legal legerdemain. They were from an old and illustrious family; the first of them to reach America settled in Connecticut in 1635 but relocated to New Jersey not long afterward.

Jehiel G. Shipman's grandfather was one of the original settlers of Morristown, and Jehiel was born in Hope, N.J., in 1818.

He attended Lafayette College for a time, eventually graduated from a college in New York, and was admitted to the New Jersey bar in 1844. His very first appearance in a courtroom was as a prosecutor of defendants Joseph Carter and Peter Parke in the infamous Changewater murder case that same year. Long before 1878, when he was appointed a judge of the Court of Chancery, his only son, George Marshall Shipman, had graduated from Princeton and joined him in practice.

A talented and articulate legal generalist, the elder Shipman was known to represent accused murderers with the same vigor and thoroughness he afforded his major financial and railroad clients. As successful as he may have been at defending railroads and banks, however, his track record with high-profile murder defendants gives one pause. Two of his most famous clients — Rev. Jacob Hardin and "Iron Mike" Bolak — went to the gallows despite his best efforts, and James Titus came within a hair's breadth of following them.

On the other hand, J.G.'s son George, educated in the classics and in practice for about a decade at the time of the Titus trial, was unquestionably one of the most distinguished young trial lawyers of the time.

As preparation for the trial progressed, the defense team was supplemented by yet another highly capable attorney, Mercer Beasley, eldest son of the Chief Justice.[12]

The defense strategy was straightforward. As the case against their client was entirely circumstantial, they would attack the weakest links in the prosecution's chain of circumstances and establish reasonable doubt in the jurors' minds. They would refute the opinions of the state's expert witnesses that Tillie had ever re-entered the Institute, that a crime had been committed on the property, even that the victim had been raped at all, by introducing contrary testimony by experts of their own. Other defense experts would establish the defendant's lack of physical capacity to commit the crime and dispose of the body. They would impugn Mead's testimony, potentially the most damaging, by attacking his credibility and portraying him as a Judas who had delivered his friend to the authorities in hope of a reward. Finally, they would call the reputation of Tillie Smith into question, since by the moral standard of the day it was considered somehow less reprehensible to rape an unchaste woman than a virgin.

As summer wore on, Titus waited in his cell in the old prison adjacent to the county Court House in Belvidere. He was treated well, even kindly, by Sheriff George Van Campen, whose charge he was, and received frequent visits from family, attorneys and friends. His confinement could hardly have been termed difficult compared to time spent in, say, New York City's Tombs, but he still was a prisoner awaiting trial on capital charges and was in close daily contact with other inmates who were habitual criminals. His jailer's courtesies notwithstanding, Titus' first-hand experience with the machinery of criminal justice must have been highly stressful, for by summer's end — when the trial was less than a week off — he appeared to be well on the way toward a nervous breakdown. The trial testimony of Titus' physician tends to support this,[13] as do allegations by the prosecution that the prisoner was contemplating suicide.

On September 26 or 27, Sheriff Van Campen discovered that a spike or similar implement had been used to remove mortar from between the bricks in a cell shared by Titus and two others. He had noticed that a large spike was missing from a nearby area a few days earlier, but when he questioned Titus about it the prisoner denied knowing anything. The damaged wall was another matter and, when confronted with the evidence Titus admitted having done some of the work on it. The sheriff, disturbed by what he regarded as ingratitude for his kind treatment of the prisoner, began a thorough inspection of Titus' cell and discovered that the tumblers in the cell's door lock had been tampered with as well.

Questioned about this, Titus first blamed a former prisoner named Holbert, but then changed the story and told Van Campen that he had done it himself, using a key obtained from fellow prisoner Edward Fuller. Van Campen angrily transferred Titus to a new cell, and returned to his examination of the old one. He next discovered a small hole in the floor, from which he extracted a hand-plaited rope 5 or 6 feet long; it had been made from a braided rug that he had allowed Titus' family to bring in to make the cell more comfortable. The only explanation Titus would offer for these irregularities was that he was sometimes half-crazy and didn't know what he was doing.

A short time later, when the trial was in progress, Van Campen searched Titus after escorting him from the courtroom and found in his pocket a second rope — a 3-foot length of sash cord taken from a window in the old jail building and twisted into a noose.

If the prisoner were contemplating suicide such proof of it, like the allegation of an attempted escape, would be interpreted as still more evidence of guilt. It seemed certain that Prosecutor Smith would present it as such to the jury.

Courtesy of Betty Jo King

Warren County Court House, Belvidere, N.J.

Warren Republican, October 1886

State Detective
John McClallen

September 28 dawned clear and bright, and every hotel and boarding house in Belvidere was filled to overcrowding. Long before the Court of Oyer and Terminer was scheduled to open, a large crowd assembled in the street outside the county Court House — most of its members seeking relief from the stale air of their lodgings, and all seeking admission to the 700-seat courtroom on the second floor.

It was widely known that the prosecution wanted to move the Titus case quickly and had asked the court to assign it first place on the list of 25 cases scheduled for argument in the fall term. Shipman & Son, attorneys of record in no fewer than 14 of those cases,[14] offered no objection. Consequently, those managing to obtain opening-day seats seemed guaranteed at least a glimpse of the defendant, and perhaps an opportunity to witness jury selection.

By 11 o'clock, even the courtroom balcony was filled to capacity, and the room was buzzing with conversation. The background noise intensity rose even further as Prosecutor Smith and the assistant prosecutor, ex-Congressman Henry S. Harris, entered, followed by defense attorneys Jehiel G. and George M. Shipman and Mercer Beasley. The attorneys sat at their respective tables, putting their papers in order, but there was no sign of Titus. Finally, the bailiff rose and cleared his throat, and the audience grew still as it focused its attention on a door to the rear of the bench, which began to open.

Chapter Four

With the bailiff's cry of "All rise!" amid a rustle of clothing and a murmuring of voices, 700 people stood. Mercer Beasley, 72 years old and Chief Justice for more than 20 years, entered and took his place at the bench, followed by associate justices Beatty, Canfield and DeWitt. After a moment, Beasley's gavel rapped, all were seated, and the day's business began. The spectators sat waiting in polite boredom for more than an hour as the court disposed of minor administrative business.

Restlessness was setting in, the clocks of Belvidere striking noon, when Prosecutor Smith finally moved the Titus case. Two jailers escorted the prisoner into the courtroom from his cell on the floor below.[1] The show had begun.

No sooner had the trim janitor settled into his seat at the defense table than J.G. Shipman rose and offered a motion to quash the second count of the indictment on the ground that it was flawed.

It was defective, he argued, because it referred to two distinct crimes, the commission of rape and the commission of murder, and because the charge of murder was not elaborated upon properly as to the circumstances in which it was committed.

The statute on which Shipman's argument was based defined first-degree murder as, among other things, bringing about death during the commission of rape. The language of the second count asserted that Titus, "in attempting to commit rape, and in committing rape in and upon her, the said Matilda Smith, did kill the said Matilda Smith."

The Prosecutor had mistakenly pleaded both the attempt and the act. Further, the allegation that rape had been committed in connection with the murder — the aggravating factor that invoked a first-degree charge — was unsupported except for an *inference* that rape had occurred.

Thus, the pleading of the second count was inadequate to

Courtesy of Betty Jo King

The Titus jury in front of the Warren County Court House — October 1886

Front row, from left: R. N. Strouse, Constable Joseph C. Thompson, Jury Foreman James Irvin Lake, William S. Pursell, Amos Fisher, Andrew B. Fritts, Samuel Reese, Reuben Eilenberger, and Constable Michael Martin.

Middle row, from left: Unidentified Man, Sheriff George T. VanCampen, Joseph Losey, Henry Y. Miller, William C. Wildrick, Milton R. Lanning, Daniel Raisley, Stephen M. Wildrick, Unidentified Man.

Back row, from left: Constables James T. Dalrymple, Charles Vass and F. J. Smith.

bring the crime within the statute. The equivalent contemporary error would be charging a defendant with aggravating conduct such as harming a kidnapping victim, a capital offense in some jurisdictions, without first establishing that the victim had been kidnapped.

Shipman argued his points for more than an hour, citing precedent after precedent, and while Beasley admitted that the count was fatally defective he was unwilling to quash it. He reasoned that Shipman's motion was unnecessary, as a charge of murder could be sustained under the third count of the indictment charging the common law crime of murder by strangulation. At the same time, he cautioned Prosecutor Smith that if a conviction did occur on the second count as worded, it would be impossible for the court to sentence the defendant on it.

Shipman took exception to the ruling, indicating his intention to make it the basis of an appeal in the event of conviction.[2] The case proceeded to jury selection.

Selecting a jury was far more straightforward in 1886 than it is today. There was no great expenditure of time, and no recourse to any expertise other than the lawyers' own. In the course of selecting the Titus jury, the court called 46 of the 48 names on a general panel of jurors: 16 were excused for cause by the defense, 10 by the court, and three by the prosecution. Five did not answer their calls. A prospective juror who was familiar with the case through the newspaper accounts could not be challenged for cause unless his mind was made up because of it.

The first day's proceedings, reported in the *Warren Republican*, indicate that just about everyone was familiar with the case to some degree, while several members of the general panel had already formed strong opinions.[3]

Despite this, a 12-man jury (women were not permitted to serve, nor were alternate jurors selected) began to take shape.

The first juror to be accepted by both sides, James I. Lake of Phillipsburg, automatically became foreman. Although his brother-in-law had served on the grand jury that indicted Titus and had discussed the case with him, Lake claimed the conversations had made no permanent impression.

Farmer William L. Pursell of Pohatcong had read about the case in the newspapers, but felt he could try it impartially, and was seated as the second juror.

The selections continued: farmer Amos Fisher of Washington Borough; farmer Andrew Fritts of Franklin; blacksmith Samuel Reese of Belvidere; merchant Reuben M. Eilenberger of Washington; merchant Joseph Losey of Washington Borough; farmer Henry Y. Miller of Harmony; farmer William C. Wildrick of Hardwick; trader Milton R. Lanning of Frelinghuysen; blacksmith Daniel Raisley of Harmony, and farmer Stephen M. Wildrick of Hope.

The New York Times observed that they seemed "above the average of criminal juries in intelligence."[4]

The entire jury selection process, including the swearing-in, was completed by the end of the afternoon, and court adjourned at 5:30 p.m.

Wednesday morning's crowds were a repetition of Tuesday's, and the courtroom was filled to capacity long before the proceedings began. Titus, his paleness emphasized by his black frock coat, sat with his attorneys on one side, his wife and father-in-law on the other. The courtroom came to order. Prosecutor Smith got to his feet, paused for a moment, and began the state's opening remarks:

> May it please the Court and gentlemen of the jury In order that you may understand this case, I must go over the facts. About October last Matilda Smith obtained service in the Hackettstown Institute. On April 8th her dead body was found about 400 feet from the rear of the building. When found it was at once evident that she had been murdered, and there had been a struggle. We shall show that on the night of the murder, Tillie Smith went to an entertainment in Shield's Hall. She was dressed in a brown dress, had on her hands a pair of gloves, carried a purse of about $6 and a handkerchief. Before going to the entertainment she went in Beatty's store and purchased a spool of cotton. After the entertainment was over, about 9:50 p.m., she and her companions crossed the street and met Annie Van Syckle, who was accompanied by Haring and Munich [sic] of Port Jervis. When they got to

the post office Tillie and Munich crossed the street and went up to the Seminary, entered the grounds and went a short way up the board walk. There they stopped and saw the lights go out. It was then 10:10, as Munich saw by looking at his watch. Tillie walked towards the rear of the Seminary and was last seen going in that direction. The articles she had purchased were gone and have never been found. There was an autopsy held and it was shown that she had died from strangulation. We shall next show that James Titus was, and had been for a long time, night janitor of the building. After closing certain doors and putting out certain lights, it was his duty to go down stairs and bolt the lower doors. He was a little late that night. He had also to go through the dining room and down stairs to the furnace room and fix the fires, and then go out and around the building to see that all was right. At that time but one person had access to the building — except the professors sometimes. We shall show you the connection with Tillie before the murder. That he had boasted that he had had, or would have, improper relations with her. He said he expected her to be away and come home late, and that he would obtain what he wished. We will show many circumstances which will add to and complete the chain of evidence — his conduct will be shown, the appearance of his coat covered with dry dirt, and his contradictory statements. In considering this case we shall produce the proofs in as near the order as the acts happened. It is not necessary to call attention to the unpleasant and responsible duty connected with this case. But we shall do our simple duty.[5]

The state planned to call 60 witnesses in approximately the same order as the sequence of events in the case, beginning with a description of Centenary, continuing with the murder, investigation and arrest, and ending with testimony by Titus' fellow inmates about his behavior while in jail. In the end, Smith called 10 more witnesses and recalled another 11 for rebuttal of the defense.

Unfortunately for the prosecutors, the content of their witnesses' testimony soon gave an appearance that the case lacked quality and their strategy was to overwhelm the jurors with large amounts of inconsequential material.

The first witnesses, a photographer and a lawyer/engineer,

National Police Gazette, October 16, 1886

James Titus faints in the courtroom on the second day of his trial.

provided photographs and engineering drawings of the seminary building.

Then, some boards that had been taken from a low platform in the basement hallway were dramatically produced by Detective McClallen; the engineer testified that he had removed them in July and kept them in his possession since. They were offered as evidence to show that the splinters found in Tillie's clothing had come from the same source.[6]

After lunch, John White, Calvin Cutler and Charles Seals told about finding the body and gave virtually identical testimony about its outward appearance as it lay in the field.[7]

Shortly after Seals took the stand, Titus became ill and had to be taken from the courtroom (it was during his removal that Sheriff Van Campen searched him and found a rope). The proceedings were suspended until Titus returned several minutes later.

Mayor Reese testified next, describing the position of the body as the others had. The board lying across the arm, he observed, was an old hemlock board, shorter than the other boards of the fence and without any indication that it had been broken from the fence recently.[8]

The last witness of the day, assistant cook Bridget Grogan, had last seen Tillie at about 6 o'clock on the evening of the murder, and did not see her again until she saw her body in the field. She had known James Titus for 11 years, and said that she had never seen him with the victim.[9]

Much of the morning of Thursday, September 30, was devoted to Coroner Jesse Smith, whose description of the body he had been called to examine on the morning of April 9 included details of its clothing.[10] He described how Tillie's underskirt had been buried with her, but was recovered by Detective Simons when the body was exhumed for transfer to the new grave.

The next witness, Tillie's roommate Stella Sliker, provided the first testimony even remotely damaging to the defendant: The last time she had returned to the seminary after hours, janitor Titus had let her in without a pass, contrary to the rules.[11]

Court adjourned at noon.

After lunch, shopkeeper George Beatty described Tillie's visit to his dry goods store shortly before the show began upstairs in Shields' Hall.[12]

Mary Wright next described her friends' walk downtown following the show, and touched briefly on their encounter with Frank Weeder and his friends in front of the Methodist church.[13] Her sister Agnes told much the same story.[14]

Annie Van Syckle, described by *The New York Times* as "the sauciest of the witnesses yet produced,"[15] described how she paid for a nonreserved seat but took a better one next to Harry Haring, and provided details of the evening spent in his company.[16]

Charles Munnich testified for the remainder of the afternoon and continued on Friday morning. The only significant testimony elicited from him was that Tillie had said she was locked out and would reenter the seminary by the laundry door.[17] This testimony, objected to vigorously by the defense, was allowed by the court and another exception taken.

Arturo Rivera and his roommate Harry Smith, while able to establish the time Tillie had returned to the grounds, were unable to provide any testimony that incriminated Titus. They had seen the victim and her escort arrive, but their vantage point was such that the window ledge blocked their view of the front and side walkways, and as Tillie drew nearer to the front of the building she disappeared from view. Neither was able to see whether she actually reentered the building.[18]

William Van Syckle, a local carpenter, testified that six or seven weeks before the murder he had met Titus at the local butcher shop, where the janitor made lewd comments to him about the new kitchen worker with whom he had taken liberties. Shipman argued that the testimony was irrelevant, and again took exception when Justice Beasley overruled him.[19]

The next two witnesses contributed little to the prosecution's case. Student James McMillan and his roommate Ted Henderson were in their room when the lights-out bell rang. Until they went to bed 25 minutes later, the two sat in rocking chairs by the window but saw nothing remarkable. Later, McMillan awoke, felt sick, and got up. While up, he again looked out his window and onto the campus, and although it was a clear night and the place where Tillie Smith's body was found was in his direct line of vision, he saw nothing unusual.[20]

More witnesses came and went: Maggie Donovan, another domestic at Centenary who had seen and heard nothing, followed by handkerchief peddler Harry Haring, who testified that he saw Munnich back at the American House at 10:45 p.m.[21]

The prosecution's case finally began to come alive on Thursday afternoon, when Dr. Whitney took the stand. On the night of the murder, he had retired between 10:30 and 11 p.m., and heard nothing unusual. He then described the duties of the janitor in detail:

Q. Will you state what the duties of Mr. Titus were that night — his regular duties were as night watchman?

A. Do you want all the duties beginning at seven o'clock?

Q. Yes.

A. Beginning at seven o'clock the duties of the night-watchman were to take full charge of the building, concerning the heating of the furnace, the looking out for the steamboilers, gas house, closing the windows that were belonging to the parlors, reception rooms, Chapel, etc., when they should be closed; ringing the first bell at 20 minutes to 10, and ringing the last bell at 10 o'clock.

Q. Where would he ring the first bell?

A. Ringing the first bell on the second or third floor on the ladies' side, then on the gentlemen's side at 10 o'clock. Then it was his duty to lock the doors that might still be unlocked — the outer doors — and lower the gas on all the halls, and close any windows that were still open, that were not windows to sleeping rooms, such as parlor windows, chapel windows, reception windows, music room windows; and then go to the cellar and attend to his furnace and the back door. *Then* he would make a circuit of the building. [emphasis added][22]

And a little later, when discussing Titus' duties after double-locking the front door:

Q. After locking the front door, where was it his duty to go next?

A. To go to the parlors, and close the windows and fasten them;

to go up stairs and lower the gas on the ladies' side of the house, on the hall, keeping the gas burning all night, but low, and then go into the top story, lower the gas there and close the windows.

Q. That was before he locked the door?

A. *The natural order would be to lock the door and then he would go down on the gentlemen's side and up on the ladies' side and attend to what I have just said, and then he would go to the cellar and attend to the boilers*, the furnaces, if they needed any attention. On the night of April 8th we did not keep steam such nights as that and probably they needed no attention — that I cannot say. [emphasis added].[23]

Q. Was there a fire in the boilers that night, or under the boilers I should say?

A. There was usually a fire in the furnace all the way along until the summer time, because we used the furnace for heating hot water, etc., for the laundry, irrespective of heating the house.

Q. Well, after fixing the fire what would he do?

A. After attending to this matter it would be his duty to go out of the back door to the cellar, to the side door, probably locking it after him by the catch lock, not the latch, and making a circuit of the building entire, to observe whether any windows had been left open on the first floor, and to observe also whether the lights were out in every room; to observe whether he saw anybody — whether he saw anything out of order, in case of fire, and he would usually make that circuit every night within 10 or 20 minutes after the first bell — the last bell — and then return to the building, locking the door after him.[24]

Whitney continued, saying he had seen Titus on the evening of April 9, less than 12 hours after the body was found, and had asked his whereabouts on the previous night. Titus had replied that he rang the first bell at 9:40 p.m., but had then been called to an upper floor to mend the caster on a bed frame. This put him behind schedule, and he rang the second bell at 10:05 p.m. instead of at 10 o'clock sharp. He then began his inside tour, locking the front door at 10:10 p.m., following which he went to the parlors and closed the windows, went upstairs and lowered the gas, and finally went down to the cellar. Then, he unlocked the rear door, made his outside tour, and returned without seeing or hearing anything unusual.

Court adjourned for the weekend.

When Whitney returned to the stand on Monday, October 4, his testimony covered conversations he'd had with Titus following the murder. His most distinct recollection was of a conversation on the morning of April 20, when he confronted Titus with allegations against him in *The World* and *The Sun*. Instead of replying, Titus pointed out the window and said there were a couple of fellows down there, a reporter and detective, and that he wished they would keep away. Looking out once again, he said they were going down the cellar and he wished they would not come around.

Later the same day, he and Titus had another conversation in the cellar. Titus had said he thought the cellar needed cleaning, and offered to have it done and the floor of the drying room swept, but Whitney said he didn't think it was necessary. Afterward he learned that, following their conversation, Titus had gone to Mrs. Ruckle and said that he (Whitney) had ordered the drying room swept, and that she should send someone to do it. Confronted with this, Titus had made no reply except to say that it seemed strange they should be looking around for hairpins because there were no hairpins in the room.[25]

Next, a conversation between Titus and McClallen had taken place in Whitney's library that same week. In the course of it, McClallen had said: "Jimmy Titus, you know who committed this murder or you did it yourself."

There was no response, and the detective repeated the accusation several times until Titus finally said: "Oh, pshaw! It's ridiculous."

McClallen made the charge once more, to which Titus answered: "I'm innocent."

Advised that someone would swear he talked to them about having taken liberties with the new kitchen helper, Titus denied having ever made such a statement.

Whitney's last significant conversation with Titus occurred a day or two later, he said, when Titus asked if he thought he should have a lawyer. He had told him he thought it was not necessary at that time, and Titus had replied, "Of course I'm innocent." Asked about his conversation with Van Syckle, in which he allegedly spoke of taking liberties with Tillie, Titus denounced it as a lie. Whitney became openly suspicious, asking whether he really thought a person could invent such a story and swear to it before a grand jury. Titus had said he believed that Van Syckle could, and then gave his own version of the conversation with Van Syckle: Having been asked by the other how things were going at the Institute, he had given some innocuous answer about there being a new young female kitchen helper who peeled potatoes. Van Syckle had replied: "Jimmy, you have got a new potato-peeler; can't you get her down in the potato cellar some time and try her?"[26] Whitney was shocked that such conversations about the Institute staff could take place, and Smith's line of questioning seems to have been calculated to elicit just such a reaction, reinforcing in the jurors' minds his characterization of Titus as a man of lewd disposition.

Witness followed witness.

Nathan Smith, Tillie's father, testified that there were bad influences in the area in which they lived, and that he had cautioned Tillie to avoid them — although his testimony didn't indicate whether she took his advice. On cross-examination, the defense made much of the fact that since his wife and Tillie had left home, Smith and his 28-year-old daughter, Kate, shared the same bedroom. The Smiths' house consisted of one large room, an adjacent kitchen, and a small storage space under the eaves, and it was hardly possible for father and daughter to have slept in separate rooms. From that point of view the entire line of cross-examination seems unfair, the phrasing of the questions implying something unwholesome about the arrangement. When asked if they actually shared the same bed, Smith denied it, adding that they slept at opposite ends of the large room. The defense's cross-examination seemingly had as its objective impugning Smith's character and, by implication, his daughter's.[27]

Elizabeth Ruckle, the seminary's matron, described a conversation with Titus in which he asked whether she thought God could forgive the person who committed such a crime. When she answered that she didn't know, he had remarked: "But the thief on the cross was forgiven." He also was reported to have remarked that although his own life hadn't been as pure as it might have been, he wouldn't commit such a crime as that.

Although this testimony implies that Titus had had something weighing on his mind — perhaps guilt — its significance was lessened by the fact that the conversation had occurred more than two weeks after the murder, at a time when the daily press was hammering away at Titus. It is neither surprising nor unreasonable that he could have made such remarks, given the stressfulness of his situation.

A particularly significant bit of testimony now emerged. On the morning the body was discovered, Ruckle had awakened at about 5 o'clock and, looking out her window, had observed two strange men walking arm in arm and talking as they crossed the Institute grounds to the rear of the main building. Such an occurrence was rare enough to be memorable. Although there was sufficient daylight at that hour for Ruckle to observe their clothing, she was unable to identify the pair except to say that they were definitely not Haring and Munnich.[28] No effort was made to develop this line of testimony further.

Matron Ruckle was followed to the stand by janitor Lewis Ayers, grocer Jacob Deremer and gardener Henry Stoddard, none of whose testimony added to the prosecution's case.

Finally, Dr. John S. Cook was called. The doctors Cook had examined Tillie's body as it lay in the field, and were later joined by doctors Ott and Johnson and undertaker Bowlby at the autopsy.

The elder Dr. Cook testified that he had arrived at the field with his son between 9:30 and 10 a.m. on April 9, and that his examination indicated the victim was then dead at least six or seven hours. He testified in great detail about the clinical aspects of the autopsy, including the subcutaneous bleeding on both sides of the head, and the condition of the reproductive organs.

The medical testimony was considered unfit for publication in any newspaper; however the trial transcript discloses not only that he found semen, but that he found a quantity apparently consistent with ejaculations by two or more men. In addition, while the muscles of the reproductive organs were described as completely relaxed and the victim was found fully clothed, no traces of semen were discovered on her undergarments. Dr. Cook considered Tillie virginal in the sense that she had never borne a child, but he was unable to render a clinical opinion about whether she was a virgin until the night of her death. Absent signs of forced penetration, he speculated that rape might have been committed when she was dead or dying, when her muscles would normally have relaxed. But he was unable to provide irrefutable clinical evidence that rape had, in fact, been committed.[29] On the following morning, Dr. Richard Cook corroborated his father's findings, as did the other two doctors.[30]

Undertaker Bowlby and his assistant Wieder next described housekeeping practices at their establishment.[31] To the prosecution's dismay it began to appear that important pieces of physical evidence — sawdust, dirt and splinters in the folds of Tillie's dress, and fragments of cane in her hair — alleged to point to the seminary, pointed with equal strength to the workroom in which the autopsy was performed. The furniture dealers' undertaking sideline was a common arrangement at a time when coffins were manufactured by local cabinet-makers. As their advertisements indicated, "(u)pholstery, repairing, and chair caning (were) neatly and promptly done" at Hackettstown's "Mammoth Furniture Establishment," along with "(e)mbalming when requested."[32]

During the autopsy, it will be recalled, both the victim's hair and clothing had been removed and deposited on King and Bowlby's workroom floor.

Dr. William Oseler, a physician and expert in microscopic analysis, offered testimony that seemed to weaken, rather than support, the prosecution. It will be remembered that *The World* reported that not only dust and splinters but stains resembling red lead on Tillie's clothing pointed to the basement room as crime scene, because pipe-fitting was done there.

Now the state's expert testified about the splinters and stains:

Q. What examination did you make of the fibres you found in the dress?

A. The fibres I examined, and they are fibres from some coniferous tree, belonging to the pine family.

Q. Did you compare them with hemlock and other pines? (Objected to as leading)

Q. Well, what did you compare them with?

A. With fibres — well, cedar, hemlock and spruce and other pines.

Mr. Shipman: I do not know if he is an expert on that subject.

The Court: Yes, he is; he says he has studied it and taught it, go on.

Witness: With reference to this I might state simply that they come from a coniferous — that is to say, one of either the spruce or pine or hemlock, but whether those are spruce or pine or hemlock I am not prepared to swear.[33]

With respect to the stains on the victim's clothes, Oseler was able to identify them as blood, urine and various vaginal secretions, but not as foreign substances. On cross-examination by Mercer Beasley:

Q. I just want to have it understood clearly about one matter, and that is about this discharge which you found upon these different articles of clothing, for instance on the red skirt, now that is purely vaginal?

A. Entirely a vaginal discharge.[34]

This testimony was significant not only for its apparent elimination of the red lead connection with the workroom, but for something implicit: There were no traces of semen on the undergarments, an important bit of evidence that would be useful to the defense.

More witnesses were called after lunch.

Niels Madsen was unable to say whether Titus had told him it wasn't necessary to come to work on the same day as the murder, or whether that was on the day before. Since the prosecution was trying to establish that Titus had set the stage for the assault on Tillie by making sure the coast would be clear, Madsen's uncertainty was helpful to the defense.[35]

The remaining testimony contributed little or nothing to the prosecution's case, and by the time court was adjourned on Tuesday afternoon the state had called 49 witnesses and had accomplished very little.

Smith now needed to pull a rabbit out of his hat. People were beginning to believe that if the testimony of Mead, his star witness, didn't bolster the sagging case, then nothing would.

The 50th witness, Thomas Howell, completed his testimony the next morning by stating that he had personally examined the covers·of the Institute cesspools because it seemed obvious that anyone acquainted with the grounds would have thrown the body there. He had wanted to see if their flagstone covers could be lifted easily, and found that they could.[36] This was another point against the prosecution.

At last, Peter Mead took the stand. The 25-year-old Mead, one-time farm manager and occasional itinerant preacher, had decided to pursue formal studies in religion two years earlier. After his second semester at the seminary, he had obtained a part-time job helping the janitors with such work as repairing chairs and wheeling coal from the bins to the furnace, occasionally even taking their places as watchman when they were overworked.

Mead testified that he had grown friendly with Titus and had conversed with him about Tillie. After relating Titus' alleged remark about "having a racket" with her, Mead told of his conversation with the janitor on the night of the murder. He testified that he had gone to the basement at about 8:30 p.m. and found Titus waiting for plumber William Drake to come by with an estimate for some steam-fitting. Titus, he said, had begun talking about Tillie Smith almost from the moment he walked in, and stopped only when Drake and his nephew arrived at about 8:50.

Mead stated that he had planned to return to his room to complete a history assignment, and had told Titus that he would not be staying around. Titus had then asked him, "Mead, are you coming down tonight?" He had replied that he was tired, had been with Titus the night before, and had a difficult history lesson to prepare. Titus had again asked him to come down, this time adding: "Tillie has gone to the show; she said when she comes there will be no one with her, then we can pump her."[37]

Mead said he thereupon exclaimed "Oh, pshaw!" and Titus again said to come down. He had been noncommittal and repeated his excuse about having to study. Then the Drakes arrived, and Mead remained another half-hour before returning to his room for the remainder of the night.[38]

Mead's direct examination undoubtedly followed his grand jury testimony point for point. At its conclusion, however, unlike that earlier appearance, he had to face the ordeal of cross-examination by Mercer Beasley. This occupied the remainder of the morning and resumed after lunch, as the two sparred: Beasley attempting to impeach Mead's credibility by trying to make him stumble when detailing all his conversations with Titus, Mead trying to look quick-witted at the defense attorney's expense.

Concerning Mead's reaction to the "we will pump her" remark, for example:

Q. Then you repeated again about your lessons?

A. Yes, sir, he said, "Come down when she comes in; she will be alone, there will be nobody with her and then we will pump her." I said, "Oh, pshaw."

Q. That was all you said, "Oh, pshaw?"

A. Yes, sir.

Q. Is that what you refer to in your direct examination as making a very short and angry answer, or words to that effect?

Mr. Harris: He said he answered with an ejaculation.

Q. Was that the angry ejaculation?

A. I beg your pardon, I have not used "angry" while I have been on the stand.

Q. Well, or words to that effect?

A. I used the word "surprise" — interjection of surprise — "pshaw."

Q. A surprised interjection it was?

A. Why, an interjection is surprise.

Q. And "Oh, pshaw" was the way you expressed it?

A. I did not say "Oh, pshaw," I said "pshaw."

Q. That was to express your surprise?

A. I said "Pshaw."[39]

Had Beasley been paying better attention, or if he had both-ered to have the transcript read back, he would have discovered that he was correct and Mead mistaken. Mead had indeed said "Oh, Pshaw!" not only on direct examination, but just a minute earlier.

More questions followed, about the time of the Drakes' coming in and Mead's leaving. Then Beasley suddenly switched gears:

Q. Do you know how many conversations you have given us here as having taken place between you and Titus, in which Titus was concerned?

A. I never counted them up.

Q. Have you never counted them up?

A. Never.

Q. Well, count them, tell us how many you have detailed to us here?

A. I never counted them. I haven't counted them, I have only given you the conversations that we had!

Q. How many is your estimate of the conversations, that you have given here today, here on the stand, in which Titus was concerned, or this murder was talked about?

A. I told you. You listened to them. I have told you all I know about it, and now you know as much as I know.

Q. No, I could not begin to tell them.

A. What are you here for?

Q. I could not begin to sit down and detail these conversations. I want to know whether you can give them to me. You are on the witness stand, you will please remember that.

A. Exactly.

Q. You are here for the purpose of answering questions, and not asking them; will you bear that in mind?

A. I will.

Q. Then I ask you the question whether or not you can tell me or that you can approximate the number of conversations that you have detailed here this morning, in which Titus was concerned.

A. I gave you all the conversations that Titus and I had.

Q. Please answer the question.

A. I can count them up if you wish.[40]

Mead then easily recounted the conversations in detail, apparently pleased with himself that he had made Beasley work very hard to accomplish very little. His small triumph was short-lived, though. By the time the court called a recess for lunch, Beasley had regained the upper hand. He continued to accuse Mead of playing detective, spying on Titus, and keeping a record of what were seemingly incriminating statements, all the while continuing to pose as the janitor's friend. With perfect timing, Beasley ended the morning session by suggesting that Mead's interest was motivated not by friendship but by the reward, and that he was no better than Judas.

The jurors would have two hours to let that sink in.

The cross-examination of Mead resumed after lunch, but if Beasley thought he had tamed the young seminarian he was mistaken:

Q. Mr. Mead, when we adjourned you had given us a list — just run over them for the stenographers to take down — of the various conversations upon this subject that you had with Titus. Do you know how many now they foot up?

A. I didn't count them.

Q. You haven't counted them?

A. No, sir.

Q. But you have run over them for us?

A. Yes, sir.

Q. And this conversation in which he tells you Tillie Smith was out, you say you were leaning against one of the pillars?

A. Yes, sir.

Q. And he was fixing the furnace?

A. No, sir, I beg your pardon, he was fixing the fire of the furnace.

Beasley had already shown signs of being impatient with Mead's jousting earlier in the cross-examination. The transcript, as impersonal as it is, captures his exasperation with the witness as examination continued:

Q. Do you seriously make that distinction; do you do it to be smart?

A. Not at all, the reason why I do that is that sometimes the furnace gets out of order, and needs repair.

Q. You didn't say that for the sake of trying to be smart?

A. Not at all.

Q. Because if you did, I beg you won't waste time over these attempts.

A. No attempts at all, beg your pardon.

Beasley continued, his voice no doubt dripping with sarcasm:

Q. When then, as you say he was fixing the fire in the furnace, you were leaning against one of the pillars?[41]

On it went, Beasley hammering away at Mead's selective memory and his note-taking, calling him a false friend and a "Judas" who sold out Titus for reward money, accusing him of acting in concert with the detectives to spy on Titus — of twisting the janitor's words.

Mead insisted that he had no interest whatsoever in a reward; that he had acted simply out of a sense of justice and public spirit.

There were no dramatic breakdowns, no sudden reversals. It simply ended in a standoff. Mead's calmness under fire must have impressed the jury. Even if his testimony didn't place a "smoking gun" in Titus' hand, it was without doubt the strongest yet introduced by the prosecution.

More witnesses followed. The employees who had helped sweep the basement room took the stand, followed by Mead's roommate, who corroborated his testimony that he stayed in his room once he returned. A postal clerk testified that Titus had asked him about state prison and how prisoners were treated there.[42]

Sheriff Van Campen described the scraping away of mortar in Titus' cell (which he admitted on cross-examination was very slight) and the ropes he had taken from the prisoner.[43] Two prisoners with whom Titus had been in jail also took the stand,[44] as did salesman Isaac Baldwin, whose testimony exonerated Charles Munnich.[45]

On Thursday morning, October 7, the state rested its case.

Chapter Five

It now fell to the defense attorneys to destroy the state's chain of circumstantial evidence by attacking its weakest links. Their strategy came down to this: Titus would be shown to be physically incapable of committing the crime hypothesized by the prosecution, and without motive. His actions following the body's discovery would be shown to have been caused by illness and stress or, equally plausible, noncriminal explanations would be offered for them. Alternative explanations would be offered for the presence of dust and splinters in the victim's clothing, and (more significantly) for the absence of other physical evidence. Mead's testimony, the most damaging offered by the state, would be weakened by portraying him as a false friend driven by the hope of a substantial reward. Finally, the emotional appeal of the case, the presumed outrage of an innocent young woman, would be blunted: Both the victim's virginity and her moral character would be called into question.

George M. Shipman rose to make the opening statement. He spoke to the jurors of their responsibility in a case built on circumstantial evidence:

> It is scarcely necessary for me to remind you of the responsibility of the occasion. A horrible crime has been committed, and you are to determine whether the prisoner is guilty. I entreat that you will weigh the case with great care. It is a purely circumstantial case. You have no right to convict upon suspicion, but you must weigh the facts. On April 9th, the body of this person was found murdered. It would be a waste of time to go over the finding of the body; how it was found, etc. But the defense will show that the prisoner at the bar is not guilty of the crime. They will show where he was, what he did, that he was weak in body, unhealthy, and even then taking medicine at the time, and was unable to have committed the crime. We will show that there was no rape committed, and if that is so the case of the State must fall. We will show you in reference to the person herself. We will show her

surroundings, and that her character was not as pure as represented. We will not attempt to dispute many of the small matters presented by the State, and which do not connect the prisoner in any
way. We will show that the prisoner had no motive in doing the
deed; that he was a man of family; had a loving wife and child;
that he was a domestic and pure man, and that he was a quiet and
reticent man, a good and true man. We will show that one or two
of the pretended conversations were not true; that he was not there
when it was said he was. We will show that he has been a worried,
harassed man from the time the girl was murdered, troubled and
watched by his false friends. We will show that he is the victim of
circumstances, which may surround an innocent man and convict
him.[1]

Titus' attorneys had decided not to let him testify, because
of his physical and mental condition, even though it was expected that the prosecution would point to this refusal as still more
evidence of guilt. Although the constitutional protection against
self-incrimination had been in effect for more than a century and
a defendant could not be forced to testify in a criminal case, the
laws of New Jersey did not prohibit a prosecutor's referring in a
derogatory way to one's refusal to take the stand. To his credit,
Chief Justice Beasley, in his charge, cautioned the jurors to draw
no conclusions from the defense's decision.[2]

The first defense witnesses, Titus' mother Rebecca and his
wife Nettie, testified about the poor quality of his health and his
general weakness, both at the time of the murder and for about
two months preceding it.

On the morning of April 9, his wife related, he had been suf-
fering from a "disorder of the liver and bowels," and came home
from his night shift looking and feeling ill. At her suggestion he
had gone to see a neighborhood doctor and returned shortly afterward with some medicine that he took before going to sleep.
He had remained in bed until nearly 4 that afternoon, although he
was awakened around noon by the voices of neighbors talking
about the murder just outside his window. He had arisen and begun dressing at that time in order to return to the Institute, but
Nettie had persuaded him to continue resting. They had briefly

discussed the news of the murder, and he had taken another dose of medicine and returned to bed.

When he awoke around 4, he washed and dressed, and spent some time playing with his daughter, before leaving for work at around 5:30.[3] The exact nature of Titus' ailment was not elaborated upon, except that diarrhea was one of the symptoms, but the implication was that it was sufficiently debilitating that he was unlikely to have had enough energy to commit the crime and transport the body as the state suggested.

On direct examination Ralph Titus, James' father-in-law, corroborated Rebecca and Nettie's testimony, but on cross-examination his credibility began to suffer. After eliciting testimony that Ralph had helped finance the defense, Smith established that he had also discussed the case with both Mead and his roommate, Horace Stout. As if that was not enough, he continued:

Q. You have talked with nearly all the people you supposed would be witnesses?
A. No, sir.
Q. With a great many of them?
A. I don't know that I have talked with any scarcely before I came down here. I could not tell you how many.
Q. Have you not talked with Dr. Whitney?[4]

Yes, Ralph admitted, he had spoken with Dr. Whitney "at different times." As Smith continued to question him, the list of prosecution witnesses to whom he had spoken grew to include plumber William Drake and his nephew, Nelson; janitor Lewis Ayers, and matron Elizabeth Ruckle. Smith made no allegation of witness-tampering, but Ralph Titus was effectively discredited as an impartial witness.

The defense was not off to a very promising start.

Blunting Mead's impact on the jury required considerable effort. The strategy was to establish that his testimony had been motivated by greed, that he had betrayed Titus and brought about his arrest by posing as his friend, and was no less willing to lie to help obtain his conviction. Concerning the latter, the defense would try to show that the most incriminating of Titus' alleged remarks, the "we will pump her" comment, could never have taken place.

Mead had survived a withering cross-examination by Mercer Beasley and had apparently impressed the jury with his composure under fire. The defense's opening salvo against him consisted of two witnesses, Thomas Howell and Joshua Curtis, who testified that he had told them about his interest in the reward. But, as the transcript shows, their testimony failed to establish any significant degree of avarice in Mead. On direct examination, Howell testified that he and Mead had spoken about the reward at his restaurant, but it developed that he, not Mead, had initiated the discussion.

The transcript shows Shipman struggling with Howell to get out the information he wanted the jury to hear — and failing:

Q. Will you state to the jury whether he ever spoke to you about the reward in this Tillie Smith matter?

A. He did, yes, sir.

Q. Now tell what he said?

A. I know that there was a reward offered of $1,000, and the talk was around, about his being the main witness.

Q. Just tell what he said, what Mead said to you about the reward and you to Mead?

A. Well, you will have it if you wait a minute.

Q. Well, we will wait.

A. I said to Mead, if he was the main witness, I should think he would go in for some of the reward or something like that; or he ought to have that reward. And he went on and said, "I think I ought to have a part of it." I guess that was about all; then I spoke about if he was the one —

(Interrupted)

Q. Never mind — well, if it was anything else about the reward said tell us that?

A. Well, if he was the one that was the means, — I guess I spoke about informing Dr. Whitney; I heard he was the first one to put them on the track.

Q. Never mind what you heard. What did he say further about that?

A. He would not say whether he was, or not.

Q. (By the Court). He would not say whether he was the first one
to inform Dr, Whitney or not?

A. Yes, sir.[5]

This could not have been the answer Shipman was expecting; it seems strange that so experienced an attorney would violate one of the most elementary rules of examination: Never ask
a witness a question whose answer you don't already know.

He quickly moved on to a second conversation only two
nights before, just after Howell had testified for the state, but appears to have done no better:

Q. What did he say to you about [the reward]?

A. I think I walked down —

(Interrupted)

Q. When was that?

A. As I left the stand here that night, that I was on for the
state...Mr. Mead turned around to me and says, "Say, did you
say anything that I said to you about the reward?"
I said, "Yes, I did."
He said, "Who did you tell?"
I said, "Told those fellows." I meant Howell Osmun.
He said, "Did I tell you?" and I said, "Yes, you did tell me."
He said, "You are sure of it?"
I said, "Yes, I am sure of it."
He said, "Will you swear to it?"
Says I, "I will swear to it."
Then he studied a while, and he said, "I think you are mistak-
en, but if I said anything about the reward at that time at Hack-
ettstown — that the reward ought to go to the state and pay the
expenses of the state," that is about all I guess.[6]

When Howell had testified for the state, his comment that
anyone acquainted with the grounds would have thrown the body
into one of the cesspools had been more helpful to the defense
than to the prosecution. Prosecutor Smith, no doubt considering
the effect on the jury of this earlier testimony, opened his cross-
examination by calling the witness' objectivity into question:

Q. You are an intimate friend of Mr. Titus' I understood you to say
when you were on the stand before?

A. Yes, sir.

Q. Are you still?

A. I am, I think a good deal of him.

Q. At the present time?

A. Yes, sir.

Q. Do you feel very friendly towards him?

A. I do; no hard feelings at all.[7]

Smith now established that during the summer Howell Osmun, a private investigator retained by Ralph Titus, had approached Howell and told him he'd heard that he was telling people about Mead's deserving the entire reward:

Q. And Howell came and told you you had said so, didn't he?

A. Yes, sir, he said that I had said.

Q. Said so and so?

A. He said that I had said that he ought to have all the reward and I said I never had said so.

Q. Has he talked with you about it since you have been here at Court?

A. No, sir, well, I saw him last night and he came in the house this morning.

Q. And he talked with you about it?

A. Well, I talked to him about lying about it.

Q. You did?

A. Yes, sir — well, I thought it was a lie.[8]

Joshua Curtis did no better. Shipman was able to establish that the witness was slightly acquainted with Mead, and that they had spoken about the reward, but as to the manner in which the subject was discussed:

Q. Did you have a conversation with [Mead] about the reward offered for the discovery of the murderer of Tillie Smith?

A. I had a conversation with him concerning the murder in which the matter of reward was mentioned or spoken of.[9]

But Mead's question had dealt not with the reward as such, but with the proper person to whom information about the crime should be communicated. Try as he might, Shipman couldn't get the testimony he wanted from Curtis:

Q. What did [Mead] say about the reward?

A. In the conversation which we had he asked me which the proper person would be to communicate any information to that one should have concerning the murder; the proper persons with whom anyone should communicate.

Q. For what purpose?

(Objected to as leading)

A. For what purpose?

Q. Well, go on and give the conversation.

A. Well, I think I am through about. I do not know what his purpose was, I do not know that he had any motive any more than a general — we had a conversation about the murder as was common anywhere and everywhere and with everybody at the time.

Q. I asked you what he said, you say he spoke about the reward? I want you to tell just what he said about the reward.

A. I think I have told you all that passed between us. It made no impression on my mind, anything that was said about it at that time.[10]

Beasley had failed to establish Mead's ulterior motive on cross-examination when he testified for the state; now, Shipman was unable to establish it through his own witnesses.

But the attack on Mead was far from over. The defense knew that Mead's most damaging testimony was the account of his conversation with Titus in the basement on the night of the murder — the "we will pump her" remark by the defendant that was being used as proof of criminal intent. Mead had testified that he and Titus were alone when the conversation occurred. The defense now attempted to show that they were not alone; that William Drake, the plumber, and his nephew, Nelson Drake, were already in the basement when Mead arrived, and were still there when he left.

William Drake's testimony was this: He had done plumbing work at the Institute on a number of occasions, was well acquainted both with the building and with Titus and, as a result of his visits, knew Mead by sight. Titus had sent word by the day janitor, Lewis Ayers, that the plumber's services were needed for some repairs to one of the boiler heads, and Drake chose the evening of April 8 to visit his client, accompanied by his 17-year-old nephew.

On their arrival, sometime between 8:30 and 8:40 p.m., he led the young fellow directly down one of the outer stairways, and along a passageway leading to the workshop and furnaces.

The Institute's three large furnaces, each with an integrated boiler, were situated in a square cement-lined pit, as it was more practical to set their foundations a couple of feet below floor level than to increase the height of the entire basement ceiling to accommodate them.

As they reached the end of the passageway, the plumbers had seen Titus down in the pit raking the fire in one of the furnaces. They had also noticed a young stranger standing in the doorway of the workshop, off to one side. The older Drake was familiar enough with Mead to know that it was not he; besides, Mead wore glasses and the stranger didn't. He turned back toward Titus to greet him, and when he looked back toward the workshop a few seconds later the stranger was gone. He assumed the young man was another of the students, and went on about his business with the janitor.

He had brought along a small model of a plumbing device he wanted to demonstrate, and it was necessary to charge it up with water at the basement sink. While he was doing this Titus came up from the pit, removed his overalls, washed his hands and combed his hair.

About 10 minutes after their arrival, Mead had appeared. All four men stood around the sink and examined the plumbing model, which Mead remarked was a good one.

Mead remained in the basement for about three-quarters of an hour, and then left. The Drakes remained there several minutes more, until about 9:45 p.m., and went directly home, a distance of two blocks.

Young Nelson Drake corroborated his uncle's testimony in every detail, adding that he had heard the Institute's clock strike 10 as he was preparing for bed a few minutes after they had returned.[11]

Here, at last, was powerful evidence against Mead's veracity, for the "pumping" conversation had supposedly taken place while he and Titus were alone together in the basement that night. If one believed the Drakes' testimony that they were in the basement before Mead arrived and remained there until after he left, he could not have been alone with Titus, and this most damaging accusation by the state's star witness would be proven false. If a witness was proven false in one matter of testimony, the law considered him false in every other, so impeaching Mead in this one matter became critical.

As expected, the cross-examination by Smith was fierce, and concentrated on discrediting young Nelson Drake who, at age 17, was assumed to be easily intimidated. He had never been to the Institute before the night of the murder, and the cross-examination included repeated questions about minute details of the basement, the type of floor, the positions of brick pillars and lamps. All things considered, the young man had a good memory and held up surprisingly well. All the little traps Smith laid — such as jumping back unexpectedly to earlier lines of questioning to see if he could catch the witness in a lie — were avoided. Young Drake stuck to his story, and the cross-examination simply petered out.

Smith would later defend Mead in his summation by mocking the "apparition" and "strange ghostly form" the defense alleged was present in the basement that night. If he existed, Smith said, surely he would have been put on the stand to contradict Mead.[12]

The next witness, Titus' mother-in-law, spoke of his reticent nature and ill health.[13]

Then, grocer Jesse Bilby testified to witnessing a prolonged conversation between Munnich, Mead and Coroner Jesse Smith in an alley behind his store immediately after the inquest,[14] suggesting that Mead was acting in concert with the prosecutors to frame the janitor.

On Friday morning, George King, undertaking partner of Frank Bowlby, testified that Tillie's hair had been deposited on a workshop floor that was frequently covered with bits of cane, splinters and wood shavings.[15] Charles Carpenter, who had wandered in during the autopsy, told how he noticed the tresses lying on the floor when they became entangled with his foot.[16] Here, the defense tactic was to demonstrate alternative ways in which wood splinters and pieces of cane could have found their way into the victim's hair and clothing.

Dr. J. Marshall Paul, who had been summoned to look after Titus when he became ill in court, testified that the defendant was in a high state of excitement, had a pulse rate nearly twice normal, and was disoriented. When Dr. Paul returned the following day, Titus had a vacant look and didn't even recognize him, causing the doctor to conclude that the defendant's state of mind was such that he wasn't accountable for himself.[17] This line of testimony was directed toward providing a reasonable explanation for the rope found in the prisoner's pocket, other than the desire of a man driven by a guilty conscience to commit suicide.

As sincere as the testimony was, and as well as it withstood cross-examination, none of it was very compelling, and the Shipmans moved into the final phase of their defense strategy: discrediting the character of Tillie Smith.

Attacking a rape victim's chastity was not only permissible but expected in 19th-century trial practice, although its benefit to the defense in this instance seems doubtful.

While the lawyers were busy defaming the victim, the monument committee, having selected a final design for a sculpture, was raising still more funds by selling small plaster models of it throughout the county.

Dr. J. Marshall Paul fired the opening volley against Tillie's virginity at the conclusion of his testimony about Titus' health. Based on Dr. Cook's autopsy report, he said, Tillie Smith was not a virgin in any sense.[18] Although there had been ample evidence of sexual contact, the private parts had shown no trace of forcible penetration.

Paul was followed by three more doctors: Comegys Paul, Henry Cox and Alvin Van Syckle. All expressed the same opinion about Tillie's prior condition of virginity, for a variety of medical reasons.[19] As their testimony dealt almost exclusively with anatomical details of female genitalia (and even included large drawings for the jurors' benefit), it was considered unfit for publication and omitted from the newspaper accounts.

One aspect of Comegys Paul's testimony, however, dealt not with virginity but with mechanics: in particular, how the location of semen found inside the victim was related to the way in which her body might have been carried to the place at which it was found.[20]

As we will see, this information might have been used to great advantage by Shipman had he not been so obsessed with pressing his attack on the victim's chastity.

In a final, almost unspeakably stupid move by the defense, three young men of questionable reputation — cousins George Sherer, Mark Dolan and George Gray — testified that they had visited a Waterloo brothel on several occasions, and had seen Tillie there. Sherer's direct testimony began by describing a house in the Saxton Falls area, just north of Hackettstown, occupied by two sisters named Mosier. The place apparently had a reputation as a bawdy house, and was frequented by the local miners. Sherer swore that he had talked to Tillie from outside the house while she was sitting inside at a window.[21]

This testimony sparked an objection by Henry Harris, since the mere fact of Tillie's having been there did not establish that she was an inmate of the place, or even that she occasionally visited it to engage in prostitution. A debate ensued, and the remarks of counsel and Justice Beasley are particularly interesting for the insight they provide into the mores and legal norms of the period:

Q. (by Shipman) State what took place there?
Mr. Harris: We object.
The Court: I don't know if that is proper excepting in a general way.
Mr. Shipman: Whether he had any conversation with her, what was said?
The Court: You have a right to show that she went to this house undoubtedly. In cases of rape, the books all lay that down. But what she did on a particular occasion is not competent. When she was

there at certain hours, or certain hours of the night you have a right
to show, or to show that she was habitually there, or there as an inmate of the house temporarily or permanently. You have a right to
show that, but cannot show what she did as a particular act.

Mr. Shipman: Cannot we prove that she was not only in the house,
but to identify her, that he had conversation with her?

The Court: You have identified her. You may ask whether he
talked with her, but not what she said.

Mr. Shipman: Cannot we prove her declarations?

The Court: You have a right to prove her declarations as to her being in the house; and in order to show that she was an inmate of
the house, what was said in that view would be evidence.

Mr. Beasley: I won't open any particulars, but in this view, anything that she said from her language, that would show in what capacity she was an inmate of the house, the character of her behavior while there and anything she said or did, that would show
how she was there, and as I said before the character of her resi-
dency there.

Mr. Harris: The authority appears to me to be the other way.

(Argument followed by counsel)

The Court: Does counsel object to what was said about why she
was there, whether she happened to be merely passing, some accident having occurred or whether she said she was not an inmate
of the house?

None of the cases deny the propriety of asking those questions.
I think that anything that she said in connection with her residence
in that house, or anything that she did while there is proper because her mere presence in the house would not necessarily imply
that she was an inmate of it for any improper purpose. She might
have gone there ignorant. She might have gone there to attend to
something that was absolutely necessary, which would imply no
impropriety on her part, or any connection with the house. If she
said "I am a resident of that house, I stay there with those girls
night and day, I am one of them" that would be competent. The
books say you have a right to show the residence in a house of
prostitution. Why not do it by the declaration of the party? You
cannot prove a woman is a prostitute unless you have someone go
there and see if she is an inmate of the house. I think you have a
right to show by her own declaration the fact that she was an in-

mate of the house, and especially declarations connected with her being there at the time. I confine counsel to declarations that tend to show her position in the house. I may say to counsel I am quite aware that the books lay down this rule in a more general form than it is applied in practice, and it has been a matter of considerable consultation with the judges as to how far that rule is to be applied; and the general impression I may say among judges is, that it cannot be enforced in the rigid form in which it is laid down. I am clear that the evidence within the limits that I lay down is admissible.[22]

As it happened, the alleged conversation between Sherer and Tillie failed to establish any reason for her presence within the limits of Justice Beasley's ruling.

The defense then took another tack, intending to show that the language Tillie used in her conversations with the witness cast doubts on her chastity:

Q. Have you had different conversations with Tillie Smith on the subject of the relations between men and women?

(Objected to)

Mr. Beasley: Our object is this — I do not mean to mention any particulars about it — but the offer is to prove that during all his knowledge and acquaintance with Tillie Smith that she would speak about the relationship between men and women.

Mr. Harris: I do not think that ought to be opened.

Mr. Beasley: I am not opening any words or anything. It is simply this, that we claim that any kind of conversation that she would hold with members of the opposite sex, in which the relationship of the sexes would be so openly spoken of and her language thereto, calling things by plain names, would undoubtedly in our opinion go to the character or chastity of the person making it.

The Court: You want to show particular instances of lewd conversation?

Mr. Beasley: No, we do not offer to prove all the different particular instances, but we offer to prove that when these matters were spoken of she would use plain terms.

The Court: If you want to prove the general character of conversation that may be competent.

Mr. Beasley: Yes, we claim this for instance — suppose you meet a person on the street, a streetwalker, and she makes some rude remark as she passes. It seems to me that would be proper, and so in this matter it seems to me the fact of a young woman carrying on a conversation with a man and calling things by their plain names would be relevant.[23]

The court eventually conceded that it would admit testimony bearing on the character of Tillie's conversation for the purpose of indicating lewdness, but would not admit testimony concerning specific conversation. Having won his point, Shipman turned to Sherer:

Q. Have you had different conversations with Tillie Smith, on the subject of the relations between men and women?
A. I do not remember ever having any conversation with her, very much, about any of her relations any more than her sisters and brothers.
Q. Well, that ain't just what I asked you. The question I wanted you to answer was, whether you and she had talked about — whether you have heard her speak about anything bad in connection with men and women?
A. No, I don't know as I ever did.
Q. Have you ever heard her speak in conversation about the private parts of men and women?
(Question objected to as leading)
Mr. Shipman: Well, I will withdraw the question. I think I am mistaken in this witness probably.[24]

Indeed he was "mistaken in this witness," and not "probably" either. His blunder was no less than the one committed with Howell, of placing a witness on the stand without being absolutely certain of what he or she was going to say.

Shipman's next witness, Mark Dolan, went as far as to say that he had spent a night at the Mosier place, that Tillie was there with the two Mosier sisters, that he had occupied the same bed as Tillie. Dolan testified on direct examination that he had removed his boots, coat and hat, and that Tillie was "undressed."[25] He had left the next morning but, curiously, was not asked by Shipman whether he had had sexual relations with Tillie.

Neither Smith nor Harris was about to ask the question, and

so Dolan left the jurors with only an implication that something had transpired. One wonders if the jurors were willing to fill in the missing spaces in Dolan's testimony, or whether they discounted it.

George Gray's testimony was no more convincing than that of his predecessors.

The final defense witness, Dr. Joseph H. Wells, added nothing to the testimony of doctors Paul, Cox and Van Syckle.[26]

On Saturday afternoon, the defense rested, and the prosecution began summoning its rebuttal witnesses, 21 of them in all, to break up the defense. Some would impeach the testimony of Sherer, Gray and Dolan, who were depicted as having poor reputations in their communities.[27] As if to bolster the rebuttal witnesses' assessment, *The New York Times* correspondent commented that when Mark Dolan was on the stand Henry Harris had elicited answers on cross-examination that would have caused most witnesses to hang their heads in shame, but that (he) basked in his notoriety. When he took his seat by a well-dressed young man, it was noticed that the latter immediately withdrew.[28]

Others, such as Lewis Ayers and Elizabeth Ruckle were recalled to tell how the Drakes had not only expressed doubts about the identity of the stranger in the basement, but had even opined that he might have been Mead after all.

Ruckle further testified that Titus had performed all his duties as usual during the two weeks preceding the murder, indicating that his weakened condition was greatly overstated.[29]

The rebuttals continued until early Monday afternoon, when both sides rested and closing arguments began.

Chapter Six

Four closing statements were scheduled, the first and the last to be made by prosecutors.[1]

With the usual formula, "If the Court please, and gentlemen of the jury," Sylvester Smith began his remarks. He insisted that the facts presented by the state proved beyond a reasonable doubt that Tillie Smith went out on the evening of April 8 with the intention of returning by way of the laundry door, and that Titus knew it. He insisted that the state had established that she was last seen on the direct route to that door and that, soon afterward, she was raped and murdered.

The evidence had shown that the crime had been committed indoors in a dry place, since the victim's clothing was covered with dried dust and splinters. The evidence, he argued, had also shown that Tillie's body had been carried to the field afterward because the murderer wanted to point suspicion away from the Institute building as the crime scene. The soil beyond the spot at which Tillie lay was soft, but there were no footprints there. The soil between the same spot and the rear of the Institute was hard — therefore the body must have been brought to the field from that direction.

Titus, who had told Mead that he would "pump" Tillie Smith, had murdered her in the basement while attempting to rape her. She had returned at 10 minutes after 10; Titus had sworn before the coroner's jury that he locked the laundry room door a little after 10 o'clock. Tillie could not have been assaulted outside before reaching the door, because residents of the Institute would have heard; therefore, she must have been assaulted after she went inside.

Smith reminded the jurors that the defense tried very hard, but had failed to contradict Mead's evidence or to show that he had base motives in voicing his suspicions about Titus. Mead, he explained, knew Titus' character and what he had said about letting Tillie in that night, and had simply told what he knew. Was it his duty to keep it a secret if he seriously believed that Titus was the murderer? When he was convinced that it was his duty to tell someone he had spoken to Dr. Whitney first, and acting on Whitney's advice, had told the detectives and the prosecutor afterward. Mead was an honest and an honorable man; the jury could believe he was alone in the basement with Titus on the evening of April 8 when the defendant uttered the incriminating remark that revealed his motive to commit the crime.

What motive was revealed? It was:

> ...to gratify the lust of the one who assaulted her. It was in attempting to commit rape and in committing rape. Was this assault done by her consent or not? When she was found, the first person who saw her saw the marks about the throat, indicating that someone had strangled her. They saw the marks on the body and blood on the hands. There is no dispute that the woman died of strangulation. The lungs had no air in them. At that moment, she was probably calling for help, and the grasping was done to prevent her shrieks. There were signs of outward violence, which would lead every one to believe that the assault was one in the commission of rape. The fibers in her dress indicate she was on her back. They indicate clearly the condition she was in — on her back struggling — and those splinters were being rubbed in, to be a silent witness of the crime.

Smith then hypothesized about Tillie's arrival in the basement just as Titus came on the scene, giving the jury this vivid, almost melodramatic description:

> Coming to the time the girl would reach the laundry door, it would have been about 10:20, or a little before the janitor came in. She would have gone in. She was probably chilly, and by stepping three or four steps she would have been in the furnace room — a natural place to have gone to get warm and remove her things, and perhaps sat down on the settee.
>
> It has been shown that she had on a new pair of kid gloves. They were new and close-fitting, and it would take some time to remove them. This she would do first. She would lay down her articles somewhere, for she had no pocket, as we have shown. Then

she would naturally take off her coat before going upstairs. He doubtless was there, or would be there, waiting for her; he would then become familiar and more familiar until there became a struggle. The old cut was torn open and began to bleed. The blood on the drawers is there evidently from the hand. She probably struggled with all her might; but he continues the struggle, and we find a blood spot on the dress, made again by that hand.

She resists until he is compelled to strike her, and she shrieks and commences to scream, and he grasps her by the throat, and again the blood spot is made on the collar by this hand. She starts to fly, and as he strikes her she falls upon those boards and he closes in on her like a tiger and accomplishes his foul purpose. He rises up, but she does not rise. There alone in that dark basement he has the corpse of his victim. He must get her away. Mead may come or someone else. He must carry her away somewhere. He would not do it roughly, but he puts down his arms and lifts her up. He carries her to one of those dusty apartments and tries to re-suscitate her, to bring her to life. God only knows what he did that lonely night.

He finds he cannot resuscitate her, and he is a murderer! What can he do? If he leaves her there it will be known by the whole world, and he will be ruined and his family disgraced. He must take her to some place which will divert suspicion from himself. He again gathers her up and takes her to the place where she was found.

Denying that Titus was ever in a weakened condition, Smith argued that he could have carried Tillie's body twice as far as the state claimed, even though it weighed more than he did.

The gloves, pocketbook, jewelry and hairpins, none of which were ever found, had obviously been destroyed by him in the furnace.

Commenting on Titus' behavior after the murder, Smith insisted that his illness and his lack of appetite had nothing to do with a medical condition, but were a confession of his guilt. His telling Niels Madsen that he need not come down to help that evening showed his intention to meet Tillie in private that night. His having the drying room swept, even after Dr. Whitney had said not to, was to see if any of Tillie's hairpins remained.

Coming to the meeting with McClallen in Whitney's office and McClallen's accusation, he had responded only "it's ridiculous," and "of course I am innocent." Was this the way an innocent man acted when accused? He had also wanted to consult a lawyer, and an innocent man would not do that either.

Mead had related how Titus walked over to a window which looked into the basement. As the investigation was then focusing on the basement, he must have been checking whether an eyewitness could have seen the murder through the window, because "a guilty man suspects everything."

Smith next dealt with the alleged escape plan and contemplation of suicide:

> Counsel will insist he was not responsible. Gentlemen, when that cord was secreted there is no pretense that that man's mind was weak, or not responsible for his actions. A writer has said that when a suspected person attempts to escape it is one of the circumstances from which guilt may be inferred. Suicide confesses. What is an attempt at suicide but confession?
>
> I am sorry to have to comment on the failure of the prisoner to speak in his own defense. The excuse is that his mind is in such a condition that he cannot answer an intelligent question. I say the conduct of this man is a contradiction to the inference of Dr. Paul. The prisoner has watched everything going on here, and you can see the interest he has had in this terrible trial, as he has watched the witnesses. We have shown, by the sheriff and constables, whom he did not know were watching him, that he appeared well enough. Even if he could only answer simple questions, he should, at least, have been put on the stand and answered such simple questions as would have been asked, to explain where he was. Ah, gentlemen, it was not safe to put him on the witness stand. There was too much to be explained. It was not safe for him to explain.

At the end, Smith addressed the defense's allegation of Tillie's poor moral character, arguing that the state had not charged that the rape was committed on a virgin. It did not matter whether she was or not. If Titus attempted to commit the crime he was equally guilty, regardless of the victim's character. All that the evidence established was that doctors will disagree.

Finally, he cautioned the jury not to act out of sympathy for Titus' wife and mother:

> If you and I are to pause at the dictates of our emotions let us not forget the lonely grave in the Hackettstown Cemetery, and let us remember that that poor girl died in the defence [sic] of her honor. In conclusion, I only wish the jury to take the testimony as presented, and if I have said anything which is not strictly in accordance with it I wish you to forget it. But I say all the evidence says to you that the murderer of Tillie Smith sits before you.

Mercer Beasley delivered the first of the defense summations. Describing the case as totally circumstantial, he begged the jury to avoid committing judicial murder, as there had been many cases in which it turned out afterward that the condemned was innocent. He cautioned them not to theorize, not to settle for probabilities, or even strong probabilities, but to seek certainties. The fatal flaw in the prosecution's chain of evidence, he said, was its inability to establish that Tillie had entered the seminary basement.

They claimed that she entered the building, citing the dust and fibers on her clothing, but never established that these were from the seminary basement. It was known, for example, that her shorn hair had been carelessly handled in the undertakers' workroom, and had even become snarled in someone's foot. Could not the sawdust and fibers have come from the workroom floor?

As for the missing purse, gloves and hairpins, all that could be said was that they weren't found near the body. There was as much reason to infer that they had been lost or stolen as there was to infer that Titus had destroyed them. He conjectured:

> Suppose she had met someone — a former lover — who was jealous, and he had joined her, and they had walked off. She might have given them to him and after that the difficulty might have occurred. She might have gone off with someone she knew — not a stranger.
>
> In a case of this kind, gentlemen, where you are asked to give this weight to the absence of these articles which the state asks you to put on it, they should have gone further and given more attention to the loss of these articles. That the mere failure to have

seen these articles at the spot should be used against this prisoner is horrible. They ask you to consider that those articles have been made away with and destroyed by this man in the heat of the furnace, and that this is evidence of his guilt, and yet they have never proven to you the loss of those articles.

That, said Beasley, was all there was in the case to show that Tillie Smith reentered the seminary and that Titus saw her that night.

Now, he turned to the testimony of William Van Syckle concerning Titus' lewd remarks about Tillie. Having read it aloud, he suggested that Titus had probably been joking, just as Munnich had been. If Munnich had been tried, the same thing would have happened to him; he would have been guilty because "his behavior showed it."

Concerning Titus' conversation with Madsen, all he had said was that he need not come down unless he wanted to. The prosecution alleged that this was evidence that Titus meant to keep him away, but they never established that Madsen would have been kept away because of it. He could have gone down if he had wanted to.

Concerning Mead's testimony, Beasley first denounced him soundly for his deceit. He reiterated the testimony of the plumbers, Drake and his nephew, which contradicted Mead's testimony about his being in the basement before they arrived.

Then, he took his parting shot at the young seminarian:

If you say they were right and Mead wrong in the very beginning of his testimony, what faith will you give to the rest? If a man is false in one thing, the old maxim of the law is that he is false in all. If a man has testified to what is not true in one respect, it is not true in any. You should take all the testimony of Mead and scrutinize it carefully and be slow to give it credence.

Now, after Mead had testified to this conversation, we pass to the next one of the conversations. You will see that Mead has gathered together every little matter — every item with a view of convicting. I wish to say that what I have said about Mead being a minister is in no way intended to cast the slightest slur on that profession. It is the noblest of professions. If I have made any strictures in this matter, it is because of what he has done in this matter — that he has lowered and degraded that profession. No man, claiming to belong to that profession, should come before the public full of deceit and false friendship. If we can show you he was deceiving and lying to Titus, as we think we can, he was doing more to degrade his profession than the vilest sinner who walks the earth. Why? Because the one acts openly and the other under a cloak.

As for Mead's interest in the reward, said Beasley, he would leave it to the jurors to figure out why he kept his written record.

Next, he addressed Titus' refusal to testify. The prosecution had said it wouldn't have been much for him to get up and say he was not guilty, but it wouldn't have ended there. Once on the stand he would have been subjected to persistent cross-examination, and every minor contradiction would have been skillfully used against him.

It would be wrong to hold his refusal to testify against him. He had told the coroner's jury all he could say; if he was innocent, he could do nothing more. In any event, in a capital case a defendant might swear to almost anything, and no jury would be likely to take his testimony seriously.

Beasley concluded:

Are you going to say because you cannot believe any other theory, you are going to accept the theory that [Tillie] went into that basement that night? I don't think a man has ever been hung on such a probability as that. The whole case is before you and you are asked to brush aside every other theory and to accept another probability, and consent to hang a man without proof. We all have a poor, limited vision, and how dangerous a theory it is to be asked to accept between two probabilities…

After the case is ended, after my colleague and the state have spoken, it will be before you to say whether this man shall be allowed to return to his child, whether his mother will have returned to her the last of her children, or whether she will lose him on the gallows.

If you convict him, it will be without proof of his guilt. We say it has not been proven, and you will find your verdict that he is a man who is innocent of this crime.

Then it was J.G. Shipman's turn. After some opening remarks about the tragic toll taken by the case on the defendant and his family, he proposed to the jury what the issue really was:

> The defendant is charged first, that he murdered this girl. Second, that he attempted to commit a rape on her and that in committing a rape he murdered her. Third, that in committing a rape he strangled her.
>
> The question here is what does the state have to maintain? The real issue is that this man attempted to commit a rape on this girl, and that in committing this rape killed her. The state does not say that he killed her with malice or forethought — or that he intended to kill her at all. So you will have nothing to do with that question — that he murdered her with malice or forethought, thereby committing murder in the first degree. The statute is that if he kills one in committing a rape, it is murder.
>
> And the state comes to you, not with direct proof. The charge of rape is hard to prove, and hard to disprove. It is a high crime, and if in committing it he takes a life, it takes his life, no matter how sorry the man may be, or how accidental it is.
>
> To prove this crime, the state comes to you with circumstances. A man may be proved guilty by circumstances, but those circumstances must be proved. They may not surmise any circumstance. Nor can they prove one circumstance and surmise the rest.
>
> Probability can never commit a man. The circumstances must all point to this one thing.

Shipman expressed surprise at the prosecutor's argument: He had merely gotten Tillie inside the seminary gate, and all the rest had been taken for granted, all pure speculation that she had entered the basement, taken off her gloves, struggled, and so on.

If the state's position was that on April 8, 1886, Tillie Smith went to a show, that Titus knew she went but arranged to let her in late, and that after admitting her he strangled and violated her, and then carried her body to a rear field, then the state was required to prove that entire proposition beyond a reasonable doubt. The jury could not convict simply because Tillie Smith was killed somewhere around the building and Titus was there.

All the defense had to do was to come before the court and

say "not guilty" over and over again until the state made out its case beyond a reasonable doubt. The defendant had already said he was not guilty of the crime; now the jury would have to decide whether the state had met its burden of proof.

Shipman continued to press this argument. The state had yet to prove the commission of a rape at all, let alone that it was committed in the Institute basement, and still less that Titus was connected with it in any way.

What had they proven? That Tillie went to a show, came back inside the yard at 10:10 p.m. What then? How did they place the defendant at the supposed scene of the crime? When the prosecutors had Tillie at the laundry door, she was more than 130 yards from Titus, who was then upstairs.

If the jurors could not find that a rape was committed they would have to find the prisoner innocent.

Because there were marks of strangulation on the victim's throat no inference could be drawn that she had also been raped, as tempting as it might be to speculate. How was it that, for all of Tillie's conjectured struggles, including the hypothetical shriek that Smith said resulted in her being strangled to silence her, no one in the building heard a sound? Tillie was a powerful young woman with strong arms; had she been defending her virtue, wouldn't she have left some mark on the perpetrator? She probably could have picked up Titus and choked him to death, yet there wasn't a scratch on him, not a rip in his clothing, not the least appearance of his having struggled with anyone.

As for the victim's purse and gloves, it was anyone's guess what might have become of them. The jury could not infer that Titus had destroyed them simply because the investigators were unable to find them. Who could say for certain that the crime had been committed in the basement of the Institute, simply because it appeared to have been committed in a dry place? There were plenty of dry places in the area, including houses, the Institute's own barn and outbuildings, and the Stewart barn, near the place where the body was found.

The condition of Titus' health was then addressed. The defendant was incapable of committing the crime. A man who could grapple with a robust woman like Tillie would need to be in good physical condition. How could a man in Titus' weakened state, a man who weighed 135 pounds, commit rape and murder after a prolonged struggle? How could he then pick up the victim's 145 pounds of dead weight as if she were a rag doll, carry it up eight steps, across a distance of 150 yards, over a fence and into a street?

And why into a street, where it was certain to be discovered, when there were two deep cesspools two-thirds of the way along his assumed path, into which he could have dropped the body without its ever being found?

With respect to Tillie's character, Shipman took full responsibility for introducing the disparaging testimony. Then he repeated all of it, adding:

> I would not take one stone from the monument to be built to the virtue of this girl, but I would say that it must be built in the right place. Would we commit a judicial murder to screen the character of this girl? They say she was strangled in defense of her virtue. She had no virtue to contend for.

But Shipman's best efforts were saved for Mead. Pointing to the young seminarian, he described him as "the most remarkable, brazen-faced, impudent witness ever on the witness stand." He continued:

> He has acted as if he knew more than John Wesley himself — what impudence! And he tells us he is an exhorter. I am sorry for it. This man is a wolf in sheep's clothing. I would counsel his church to attend to him. Why, gentlemen, a Benedict Arnold or a Judas Iscariot would turn away from him. The people of God are against a liar, and what was this Mead doing but acting a lie all the time? I would advise him to go and read carefully the 55th Psalm[2]— to read and study it.
>
> He was astonished because he found this poor fellow reading the Psalms of David. And they want to infer that he is a murderer because he did this! A great many good men have gone to the Psalms for consolation. But Mr. Mead thinks because this poor fellow did so, he was a murderer.

There had been a reward of $1,000 for the discovery of the one who did this deed. He was first in the field. He went to Mr. Curtis and Mr. Howell and asked about the reward, and that he thought he ought to have half of it. Of course he had to deny it, but Mr. Howell says he did say so, and Mr. Howell's testimony stands unimpeached. This overthrows all his testimony.

And what does he admit on his cross-examination? That he was a spy, a spy on his friend. I have never in my life seen anything so degrading. He ought to be hooted out of the church. He acted a lie all the time, and he is just as much of a liar as if he had spoken a lie.

The jurors were reminded that Titus had consistently protested his innocence. Concerning the attempted escape, Shipman claimed that the two informers had concocted the story to curry favor with the authorities and expected to gain their freedom by testifying against the defendant. If there had been an attempt at suicide, the strain of confinement and the impending trial had caused it:

...his mind was broken down. The learned counsel says, "Suicide is confession." This might be if he was in his sound mind. He is the son of a father who took his life. With his nerves broken up and his mind destroyed, he thought to do what his father did. Will you visit him with criminal affliction, with stripes and the halter, because he has inherited this trait from his parent?

True, the defendant had not taken the stand, but even if he had some would still say he couldn't be believed because it was a capital case and he was swearing for his life. The laws of Pennsylvania and New York provided for mistrial if a defendant's failure to take the stand was alluded to by counsel. The same was, unfortunately, not true in New Jersey, and the jury should refuse to draw conclusions simply because the prosecutor had taken advantage of the opportunity thus provided.

Finally, the jury was thanked for its attention, and this closing remark added:

I have seen the friends of this man — his wife, his mother, and they have always said — "Take good care of James," and we have taken good care of him, the best we could. His little pittance is gone, and now we plead for you to save him his life — all that is left him.

We plead for mercy. They say there is no mercy in the jury box. But mercy is here, too, and will speak. I commend him to you and bid you farewell.

The final summation was by Henry Harris.

Describing man's lust as "a potent force," he gave numerous historical examples of ruin brought about by it. Members of the jury were there in the interest of protecting their own wives and daughters, to determine whether the defendant sacrificed the life of Tillie Smith to his unhallowed lust.

Dismissing the argument that a defendant might be wrongly convicted on circumstantial evidence, Harris asked the jury to consider the following:

We find Titus was of a lewd disposition long before this murder. We have heard of the conversations he had with Van Syckle and Thompson. Next, he had an opportunity to commit this crime. He knew she had gone to the show and he knew she would come in through the laundry door. You have these. Having this disposition it is a fair inference that he had a motive toward the girl.

Next, the time. Munnich and Tillie went up the street and went 15 or 20 feet in the yard. The lights went out and the door was locked. It was 10:10. She left him declaring her intention of going to the laundry door, where Titus was. They must have met there. There is a discrepancy of a minute in the time when she was to get there and when he got there.

Harris' remarks essentially restated Smith's. The Drakes' testimony was dismissed as unbelievable. Titus did not protest his innocence strongly enough ("would any man have sat silent under such dreadful accusations as that?"). It was always considered an admission of guilt when a man attempted to escape, and Titus had made the attempt. Tillie's character was attacked, yet she had the respect of all for whom she worked. Here, he read Titus' own statement at the inquest: "She had a very good character."

He continued:

Her dead body tells you her character was good. Her dead

body tells you she had been raped and killed in the commission of the rape. This is proof of her character. They say he was not able to do this deed. But he could. He heaved the coal and carried the trunks from the top to the bottom of the building.

Matilda Smith is not a figure in this scene. From her lonely grave no voice can come, no sound above the murmur of the autumn winds above it. If she could come back and revisit the glimpses of the moon, I fancy her voice would not cry out for vengeance, great as is her wrong, but with suppliant hands she would, gentlemen of the defense, say: "Spare the memory of my good name."

The state of New Jersey, he proclaimed, did not seek vengeance, but only to vindicate the majesty of its laws, and to keep its citizens, their wives and daughters safe from murderous rapists.

He concluded by challenging the jurors to decide who killed Tillie Smith:

Was it not the man who acted lewdly toward her, who had lascivious intentions toward her?... Was it not him who prepared the way to receive her — who lied as to the time he ordered the coal; who, when he heard of the murder, remains silent in his room, and gave no information to the authorities as to her remaining out all night;... Was it not the man who lied to Mrs. Ruckles as to Dr. Whitney's order to have the drying room swept and connected it with "hairpins?" Was it not a man in a dry place where there was coniferous wood, where there was dry dust? Was it not a man who feared suspicion and who laid her hat and cloak and collar with her? Was it not one who must get her off the Institute premises? Was it not the man who spoke of forgiveness for such a crime — who spoke of the immortality of his soul, in connection with the crime — who found much comfort in the Psalms? Was it not the man who inquired as to treatment in state prison? Was it not the man who dug the jail wall — who engaged in a conspiracy to break jail, involving violence; who threatened Mead with death; whose cell contained two ropes before any pretense of mental incapacity is made, on the day of the removal? Is it not the man who was found with a noose in his pocket, either for self-destruction or for a sham to cover the incident of the other rope? Is it not the man who, while claiming to be innocent, still finds it necessary to slander the dead girl's memory?

Is not James J. Titus the man who murdered Tillie Smith? There he sits with silent, attentive gaze, but silent as his victim in the tomb.

The lawyers' work was complete. Justice Beasley issued his charge to the jury. He went to great lengths to define the rules governing circumstantial evidence and reasonable doubt and, to his credit, admonished the jurors to disregard all remarks concerning Titus' refusal to testify in his own defense.

Then he addressed specific portions of the testimony, and identified for the jurors the issues they would have to resolve. For example, whether someone familiar with the seminary might have been expected to conceal the body in the cesspool, whether it was believable that Tillie had entered the building, and so on.

The charge complete, the 12 jurors were escorted to the jury room to begin their deliberations.

They deliberated for two full days. At 6 o'clock Friday morning the ringing of the courthouse bell announced that a verdict had been agreed on, and the streets filled with people hurrying to get to their seats.

The chief justice arrived first, then Prosecutor Smith, and finally J.G. Shipman, whose back yard abutted on the courthouse. The jury was summoned and filed in solemnly, indicating what the verdict was likely to be.

Titus was brought in last, looking very upset and evidently suspecting the worst.

The clerk of the court spoke: "Prisoner look on the jury; jury look on the prisoner. Gentlemen, have you agreed on a verdict?"

The jurors answered in unison: "We have."

"Who shall say for you?"

"Our foreman."

The clerk now turned to Foreman James Lake, and asked: "Do you find the prisoner guilty or not guilty as charged in the indictments?"

Perhaps it was the awesome realization that his next few

words were going to bring about another person's death that made Lake nearly gag as he tried to get them out. He struggled to control his voice: "Guilty of mur…"

But the strain proved more than he could handle, and he paused, choking on the word with a sob, then finally blurting it out: "…murder in the first degree." He then collapsed into his seat.

Titus received the verdict without apparent emotion, and Shipman demanded that the jury be polled. Some of the members seemed so overcome by the emotion of the moment that they could not utter the word "guilty," and simply nodded their heads.

The trial was over. Chief Justice Beasley discharged the jurors after thanking them for their service, and the prisoner was returned to the county jail to await sentencing.[3]

The Shipmans filed an appeal by the end of the day. Besides the matter of the defective indictment, which had been raised at the opening of the trial, they learned that during deliberations the jury had sent out for magnifying glasses, without the court's knowledge or permission, to examine the splinters in Tillie's clothing more closely.[4] A jury is supposed to consider only the evidence presented in the courtroom, and an unfavorable evidentiary discovery made in the jury room can result in a mistrial if taken into account in the verdict.

The appeal was drafted in the form of a "show cause" motion requiring the state to show why Titus should not be granted a new trial. Chief Justice Beasley approved the motion and scheduled argument for the Appellate Court's November term; Titus would not be sentenced until the issue was decided.

A few months later, in one of those curiosities of the legal process, Beasley, who was also chief justice of the Appellate Court, ruled on the motion that had come up from his own lower court, instead of disqualifying himself. While sustaining the defense position on the defective indictment, he favored the prosecution on the matter of the magnifying glasses, deciding that their use could only have strengthened the defendant's case and was therefore not prejudicial.[5]

The Shipmans' appeal was dismissed and sentencing scheduled, first for January 4, 1887, and then for January 24.

Despite a snowstorm, the courthouse was crowded to capacity on sentencing day. Chief Justice Beasley and associate justices DeWitt, Canfield and Beatty were on the bench, and the bar was crowded with attorneys and others who had been involved in the investigation and prosecution.

Titus was brought from his cell, neatly dressed in black and looking in good health. After being seated, he chatted casually with J.G. Shipman and relatives.

A hush fell as Prosecutor Smith rose and stated that the records in the case of James J. Titus had been returned from the Supreme Court and moved that sentence of death be pronounced as provided by law.

Shipman sat quietly looking over the case records as the clerk of the court, at the chief justice's instruction, ordered Titus to stand. In response to the usual question about whether he had anything to say before sentence was passed, Titus replied that he did.

Standing erect and speaking in a loud, clear voice, he calmly declared:

> My counsel have said in my defense all that can be said. But I wish to make one or two remarks for myself. I have to express my regret that upon my trial I was unfitted both mentally and physically to be a witness in my own behalf. I am of a low and despondent turn of mind at all times and this feeling coupled with the close confinement to which I was subjected entirely broke me down both in mind and body.
>
> Since my trial, owing to the kind and gracious treatment of the sheriff allowing me freely to walk out in the corridor of the jail, I have been much improved in mind and body. And now I wish here to protest, before this court and before the world, against the conduct of the jury that tried me.
>
> They tried me in my absence and falsely convicted me of a crime of which I declare here and now in the presence of this court and my countrymen who now hear me that I am not guilty.
>
> And I most humbly ask the court to spare my feelings by sentencing me in as few words as possible, as nothing the court can say about the crime of which I am convicted can apply to me, as I solemnly repeat I am not guilty of it.
>
> These are all the remarks I desire to make.

Then, turning to the chief justice and calmly folding his arms, Titus said, "I am now ready to hear the judgment of the Court."[6]

No power on earth could have deterred Justice Beasley from delivering a suitable homily. After briefly stating the history of the case, he directed his efforts toward impressing upon Titus the importance of fully realizing the enormity of his offense:

> ...for that is the first step toward repentance. You should bear in mind that it is only as a penitent that the guilty man can ask for mercy from that All Wise Being before whose judgment seat there is every reason to believe you are shortly to appear. The only effect of your denying your guilt is to aggravate it and to harden your own heart, for no one fully acquainted with the history of your case and its developments doubts but that you did most barbarously kill this young woman, that you laid in wait to get her in your power, and then either in the gratification of your brutal passion or to conceal the crime induced by it, you murdered her.
>
> By that terrible deed you broke the law ordained by man and for that crime you are about to suffer the penalty. By that same act you broke the law of your Maker, whose judgment awaits you beyond the grave, and I advise you to use the short time that will be given to you in the endeavor to obtain by true and unfeigned penitence for forgiveness of your great sin from that All Merciful Judge who doeth all things well.
>
> Do not delude yourself by vain hopes, but at once seek the aid and counsel of those whose sacred office it is to assist all who are in trouble and in danger of death.

Finally, he arrived at the part for which the spectators were waiting:

> The sentence of the law is, and the court does here adjudge, that you, James J. Titus, be returned to the jail whence you came, there remain in close confinement until Thursday, April 14 next, and that on that day you be taken thence to the place of execution to be provided by the sheriff of this county, and then and there on said day, between the hours of ten in the forenoon and two in the afternoon, you be hanged by the neck until you are dead.

The Chief Justice paused a moment before adding: "And

the defendant guilty in manner and form as
he stands charged in the Indictment or not guilty,
say by their foreman that they find the defendant
guilty of Murder in the first degree" and the jury
being poled at the request of the defendants
Counsel, so say they all,
The prisoner was then remanded to jail until
January 4th 1887 to receive his sentence
January 4th The prisoner was again called at the
bar and remanded back to jail till January 24/87

Jany 24/87 — The prisoner being again placed at the bar to
receive his sentence, the Court do order and adjudge
that he be taken to the jail from whence he came
and there safely keep until Thursday April 14
AD 1887 between the hours of 10 A.M. and 2 P.M.
of said day and that he be hanged by the
neck until he be dead dead dead,

Jany 24/87 — By order of the Statute in such case
provided the Courts here appoints and designate
the following persons who are Inhabitants of
the County of Warren and liable to duty therein
as grand Jurors and who are respectable persons
and two of whom are Physicians to be present
and the time and place of the execution of the
Judgment rendered in this case and to attend
upon and witness the same that is to say,
Dr. J. Marshall Paul, Dr William H. McGee
Richard D. Drake, William M. Maberry Howard
Mullick. Sharp Mullick John H. Hildebrant
John A. Wildrick. Henry Woolverton Hen...
Johnson Thomas Kearnly, Samuel Johnson
In witness Whereof we have hereunto set our
hands and seals this 24th day of January 1887
        M. Beasley
        J. H. Dewitt
        Geo A Beatty   Judges
        H Canfield

Courtesy of the Office of the Warren County Clerk, Belvidere, N.J.

Minutes of the Court of Oyer & Terminer for January 24, 1887,
recording the sentence that James Titus be "hanged by the neck until
he be dead dead dead," and appointment of official witnesses to the execution.

may God have mercy on your soul."[7]

The *Hackettstown Gazette's* reporter noted that there were few dry eyes in the crowd at the conclusion of the judge's remarks, and that the condemned man was one of the exceptions. Titus appeared to be the least concerned person in the room as he took his seat while friends and relatives crowded around him.

In a brief interview with a newspaper reporter, he said he did not have a fair trial and thought, with the popular feeling so strong against him, that a fair trial was impossible.

There would be one more appeal, to the Court of Errors and Appeals, beyond which the only hope of escaping death would be a Court of Pardons' commutation of sentence to imprisonment for life.

The court next appointed 12 people to serve as witnesses to the execution.[8]

Titus was returned to jail to await the hangman. Sheriff Van Campen was directed to keep a constant watch over his prisoner, day and night.

Chapter Seven

Spring came, and with it the astounding news that Titus had escaped the gallows and had been sentenced to life imprisonment at hard labor after confessing his guilt. A *Times* article had noted a month before that interest in the case was reviving:

> Public opinion, which during the progress of the trial was strongly against Titus, is reacting, and today many think the extreme penalty of the law should not be inflicted. This case will be memorable in Jersey jurisprudence as showing the minimum of purely circumstantial evidence required to secure a conviction for murder. Many think there were weak links in the chain woven by the prosecution and who doubt the justness of the verdict.[1]

Petitions for commutation of his death sentence had begun circulating almost from the day it was pronounced, and had been well received. Among the signers were 11 of the trial jurors, 23 of the 25 lawyers comprising the Warren County Bar, and most of the Legislature.[2]

But as successful as the petition drive was, the decisive factor was a confession by Titus in the form of an affidavit to the Court of Pardons in which he retracted his plea of innocence and his statement to the court at sentencing. All appeals having failed, the Shipmans had reportedly wrung from him the true story of the crime which, it appeared, had occurred in circumstances amounting only to second-degree murder.

The Court of Pardons remained silent about the content of the affidavit and its own decision-making process, but *The New York Times* and the *Hackettstown Gazette* went to press with the details within a day of each other.[3]

Titus claimed that during the trial he had been overcome by sickness. Medical testimony had established that he was unfit to take the stand and tell a coherent story, thus he had not presented his confession to the trial court so that it could be subjected to

cross examination and rebuttal. The *Gazette* gave this account of
the confession:

> It sets forth that Tillie was not the chaste girl she was supposed
> to be; in fact, Titus acknowledges that he had been unduly inti-
> mate with her from the time she first entered the Institute as a do-
> mestic. He states that on the night of the murder, Tillie Smith no-
> tified him that she was going to the show which she attended and
> that she would not be in till late, and wanted him to let her in when
> she returned. He told her to go to the matron and get permission,
> but she refused to do so saying it was against the rules. After per-
> suasion he consented to wait for her and let her in. She then went
> with him to the engine room and sat on a settee and began taking
> off her outer wraps and gloves. Titus banked up the fires and then
> left her for a few moments and made his usual round, as sworn be-
> fore the coroner's jury. He returned about 10:30 and found Tillie
> waiting for him, who consented to every proposition made her
> and offered no resistance whatever. Titus claims this meeting was
> a prearranged one and with a full knowledge on her part of its im-
> port, the occurrence transpiring in the same room on a robe spread
> on the floor. She afterwards communicated to him her fears that
> she was in trouble, from which he endeavored to dissuade her, not
> successfully however, and she finally told him that if such should
> prove to be the case, she would expose him as the author of her
> ruin. He protested against that course and she insisted on it till, as
> he says, he in anger grasped her by the throat and held her for a
> moment. He heard a gurgling sound, and thinking that something
> serious had happened went for a light, and when he returned
> found that she was dead and had fallen from the sitting posture
> she was in to the stone floor, causing those bruises on the head so
> puzzling to the physicians in the case.[4]

While the confession confirmed the state's suspicion of Titus as the killer, it called into doubt both premeditation and rape,
either of which was essential to sustain a capital murder charge.

The Shipmans pressed this argument, and the Court of Pardons recognized that there was now a reasonable doubt that murder in the first degree had been committed. In commuting Titus'
sentence to life at hard labor, they gave him the benefit of it.
Commentators later observed that if he had admitted the killing

and denied the rape at the outset it would have made a great difference in the outcome. Instead of barely escaping the gallows and receiving a life sentence, he would have been liable to a 20-year sentence at most.[5]

There are conflicting reports about the manner in which news of the commutation was received. According to the *Washington Star*:

> [It] was accepted with almost universal joy throughout the county. While very few doubt Titus' guilt, hardly a person desired to see him executed on evidence of so circumstantial a character. "I am glad of it," says everybody.[6]

The *Belvidere Apollo* indicated that there were numerous and widely differing opinions held, examined the range of them and made few other comments.[7]

In Hackettstown, where support for a native son had been strongest, reaction to the confession and commutation would be most pronounced. It ranged from embarrassment among the petition-signers, to disbelief (the confession conflicted in many ways with the known evidence), to outright anger.

However, an equally troublesome aspect of Titus' affidavit appears to have been its conflict with the popular belief in Tillie Smith's unblemished character and death in defense of her honor.

The Sun, in an article detailing a number of short interviews with Hackettstown's leading citizens, attempted to show the extent of their outrage:

> Thomas Shields Jr., one of the most prominent merchants of the town, says: "I have not yet read the confession, but have had it explained to me, and am more than surprised at the action of the Court of Pardons in view of it. I signed one of the petitions for the commutation of sentence because I was not satisfied at seeing a man hanged upon circumstantial evidence. His story of the murder and the cruel way in which he attacks his victim's character has put an entirely now face on the matter, and I am very sorry now that I signed any petition."
>
> "Do you think that the Court of Pardons erred in their decision?"

"I most certainly do, and I think they are deserving of censure. How they could have interfered in his execution after reading that confession is more than I can comprehend."

"Do you believe that the confession is a correct statement of the way in which the murder was committed?"

"I do not. I believe it to be a lie framed at the instigation of his lawyers for the sole purpose of saving his neck. No one here believes that Tillie Smith was unchaste, and they certainly will not alter their opinion because of the affidavit of a confessed murderer. I think that the Court of Pardons owe it to the people of New Jersey, and particularly to those of this section, to publish the confession in full and the reasons for their action.

I hope that the press will voice the sentiments of the people in this matter and will demand an explanation From the Court of Pardons in such a way that that body will not dare refuse it."

Mr. Shields, continuing, said that he had heard opinions expressed by dozens of his townsmen, and that with few exceptions they thought as he did.

Mr. Augustus Cutler, ex-councilman and a leading citizen, and who was one of the witnesses for the state, is very bitter in his denunciation of the Court of Pardons' action. He was satisfied from what he knew of the case that the alleged confession of Titus was a tissue of lies, particularly in regard to the attack on Tillie Smith's good name. In his mind the commutation of sentence was an outrage. Either Titus was guilty or innocent of a foul murder. If innocent he should be freed; if guilty he should be hanged.

Mr. J.G. White, who is connected with the New York Electric Light Company, and who is personally acquainted with two of the pardoning Board — Judge MacGregor and Gov. Green — said he was greatly surprised that anyone could have considered favorably a recommendation for the murderer's commutation after hearing the evidence in the case. He did not see how this Court of Pardons could have arrived at their conclusion, and most earnestly hoped that their reasons would be made public.

Mr. D.P. Cole, the father of the Cashier of the Hackettstown Bank, and an elder of the Methodist church of which Titus was a member, said that he could see no excuse for the Court of Pardons taking the view they did, especially after reading the confession. That was sufficient to satisfy any man that Titus was not only guilty of murder but also of assault. In his opinion the confession was the most damning evidence of the murderer's guilt which had appeared.

John R. Carr, the Town Treasurer and Tax Collector, failed to see how the Court of Pardons could give any reasons for their act. He thought they were deserving of severe censure from the people of the state.

Mr. M.R. Nunn, who has been City Assessor for twelve years, and who is a trustee of the Methodist Church, signed the petition for Titus's commutation of sentence because he thought it just possible that the man was innocent. Since reading this confession he no longer had any doubt of Titus's guilt, and could see no reason why the Court had acted as they did.

"If I had an opportunity," he said, "I would sign a petition now to have Titus hanged."

John Dill and Daniel Vliet, the latter a director of the Sussex National Bank, drove into Hackettstown yesterday from Hope, which is about twelve miles distant. They reported that farmers around Hope and in other sections of Warren County were very bitter in denouncing the injustice and imbecility of the Court of Pardons in their action. The more outspoken and impetuous citizens of the county say that they only regret that lynch law cannot step in and settle the matter. One respectable-looking old man, who said he did not care to give his name, expressed himself in this wise. He said: "D___d if I wouldn't like to see Lawyer Shipman and the members of the Court of Pardons put in Titus's place, and Titus turned loose here in the town where we could get at him.

We'd soon show the country that Jersey justice was not dead yet."

This sentiment met with the hearty approval of the crowd of bystanders.

"That's the talk," said one. "That's how we feel."

It was said over and over again that if the victim had been a young lady student, or, indeed, anyone except a servant maid, Titus would never have gone to prison for life. In that event he would have been hanged long ago.

Thomas Brandt, an elder of the Presbyterian Church, smiled grimly and said:

"Let them pardon him and send him here. That is all we want."[8]

The reaction elsewhere in the county was said to be similar,

115

but although *The Times'* correspondent in Belvidere reported receiving a telephone call from nearby Phillipsburg describing crowds of angry and excited laborers congregating in the streets and discussing the situation, nothing seems to have developed beyond idle talk. With the weekend approaching, Sheriff Van Campen asked the authorities if it was necessary to call up an extra posse to guard the county jail, and was told it wasn't. Although the Court of Pardons allowed the sheriff 10 days' time to deliver Titus to Trenton, he decided to take no chances and took him there by train in the early hours of Saturday morning.

Surely relieved finally to have such a high-profile prisoner off his hands, Van Campen expressed the opinion (according to *The Sun*) that there might have been trouble had he kept him in the county jail over Sunday. But *The Sun's* reporting needs to be taken with several grains of salt, recalling the boast that its efforts had pushed the investigation in Titus' direction in the first place. More to the point, *The Sun* was "scooped" on this occasion by none other than the *Hackettstown Gazette*, which for all its small-town flavor had put out the details of the confession before any of the big New York dailies.

In a classic sour-grapes shot at the competition the *Gazette* was derided as "published by the Rittenhouse Brothers" and having "...always been a sort of semi-official organ for Titus' counsel, Judge Shipman..."[9]

Having vented his frustration, *The Sun's* reporter turned to the future of Tillie Smith's memorial:

> It is thought that the present excitement will do much toward awakening renewed interest in the Tillie Smith monument fund. The people believe that she was chaste and honest, and the attempt to blacken her reputation causes great indignation. The fund now amounts to about $700, and it is hoped that $1,300 more will be soon raised.[10]

That hope was soon realized and the monument was unveiled on a raw November morning in 1887 before a crowd of 600, a monument to life presumed lost in the cause of chastity.

A homily was delivered, and prayers were offered as a brass

band played hymns and dirges in the background. The leaden sky and intermittent downpours seemed perfectly suited to the occasion, and from what has been told of it in the newspaper accounts the spectators' eyes were as damp as their clothing.

Dr. Whitney addressed the gathering, and after giving a brief history of the crime and the conviction of Titus, reassured the gathering:

> Throughout the months between the murder in April to the trial in October, and throughout the twelve months that has [sic] passed since the trial, notwithstanding the criminations of the guilty man against his victim, the committee wish to say to the public that nothing whatever has transpired to shake their most implicit confidence in the virtue of the unfortunate Tillie Smith. Your speaker has thus chosen to be explicit on this occasion because he was the employer of this girl, because he is a member of the monument committee, and because up to this hour your committee has made no public utterance whatever on the subject. And, besides, it is due to the generous contributors to this work, as also to the widely interested public, that they should know that their committee has had and still has unwavering faith in the innocence of the victim of this foul crime.

He went on to thank the people involved in raising the monument: the committee, the public, the newspapers and the stonecutters. Then, as the final step in the apotheosis of Tillie Smith, he concluded:

> Today we unveil this beautiful memorial, erected to the memory of one who was worthy of the high honor. The last three months of this young woman's life, the period which specially represents our more intimate knowledge of her character, we find her uniformly faithful in the performance of every duty, respected and highly esteemed by her employers and companions. Conversing often with her friends on religious subjects; never absent in the evening, save on that last unfortunate night, except to attend church services, this young girl always gave evidence of striving to be a true woman, thus ever proving herself worthy of the confidence she won; and at last, when the awful struggle came, preferring to give up life rather than honor. This elegant monument is

Hackettstown N.J.
June 13th 1887

To the most Honored counsel
of the City of Hackettstown
Your Honor As there has
bin a reward of $1000.00
Dollars offered to any person
or persons, who would give
evidence that would leads
to the conviction of the
murderer of Matilda Smith,
who was killed on April 8th
1886 I Peter F. Mead of said
place bring the person who gave
the evidence which convicted
the murderer of said
Matilda Smith claim said
reward or part there of as
your honorable body deem
I justly deserve, on

I remain
Peter F. Mead
Hackettstown N.J.

Peter Mead's letter of June 13, 1887, claiming the reward.

of granite, typifying the strength of virtue in every true woman's heart. This sculptured maiden, standing out in bold relief, clad in Grecian drapery, holding up the chaplet of oak leaves, represents all that was strong and noble in the older civilizations; for nothing is more true in the histories of Greece and Rome than that the nation was mighty and dominant only when: "Caesar's wife must be above suspicion;" only when the charmed circle of home was presided over by the purity of the Grecian or the Roman matron. When woman fell, or when man ceased to reverence woman as wife, or mother, or sweetheart, then the nations fell. Virtue alone is strength in man, in woman, in empires.[11]

It is not recorded whether he saw any symbolism in the graceful figure emerging from a hard, rough background. At the close of his remarks the band played another dirge, and the ceremony ended with a benediction.

A few weeks after Titus was sent off to state prison, Mead had written to the Hackettstown council claiming the reward.[12] It is not known whether he received it, but what is known is that he did not remain in Hackettstown beyond 1887. In reply to a Centenary College survey of former students in 1917, he wrote that after leaving the Institute he completed his theological education at Drew University, was ordained in the Methodist ministry, served in both the Newark and Wyoming conferences, and was currently retired. An inquiry at the Methodist Archive at Drew verifies that Mead graduated and served in those conferences, but that he later left the denomination's active rolls "for reasons other than retirement," giving us yet another reason to wonder about his veracity.

J.G. Shipman died less than 10 years later, but his descendants continued to practice law in Belvidere until the 1970s.

Centenary Collegiate Institute burned to the ground on October 31, 1899, and was rebuilt as Centenary College within three years. Its cornerstone, all that was saved from the ruins, was reset into the foundation of Seay Hall, which now occupies the site.

As for Titus, he never saw his wife again after he left for prison. She died in November 1904, shortly before he was paroled, and his daughter Lizzie, then nearly 21, went to Trenton

State of New Jersey,

Trenton, July 9th, 1902.

No.

To the Honorable THE COURT OF PARDONS:

The undersigned will give employment to James J. Titus now confined in the State Prison at Trenton, if paroled.

My post office address is Hackettstown, N. J.

Business Caterer and Restaurateur.

Thos. B. Howell

APPROVED Franklin Murphy Governor.

State of New Jersey,

Trenton, Dec. 27, 1904.

No.

To the Honorable THE COURT OF PARDONS:

The undersigned, Principal Keeper of the New Jersey State Prison, hereby certifies, that James J. Titus convicted of the crime of murder at the County Court of and now confined in the State Prison, has been a good prisoner, and is, in his judgment, a proper person to be paroled in accordance with the provisions of Chapter 231 of the Laws of 1891.

George O. Osborne

Keeper

James Titus was paroled by the Court of Pardons on December 27, 1904, having served 19 years in prison.

Titus' friend Thomas B. Howell filed this promise of employment, dated July 9, 1902, with the Court of Pardons. This fulfilled one of conditions leading up to his parole.

with friends to bring him back to the town of his birth. The approval of his parole only a few days before Christmas was barely noticed outside of Hackettstown,[13] but in the *Gazette's* words:

> His coming back to the world after a term of nearly nineteen years of close confinement was without sensational features. He went in a stalwart young man of 34 years, and comes out an old man at 53, broken in health and spirits. One or two gentlemen from Hackettstown were with him in the prison when the Court was considering his case. It was presented and mercy urged by Governor Murphy, who had taken a great interest in all the details. Keeper Moore, of the State prison, who had urged clemency and who firmly believed that all the ends of justice had been met, was at his side when the telephone rang and the action of the Court was announced. Turning to Titus, with tears in his eyes and voice, he said, "Jimmie, what do you think of that for a Christmas message?" "They are the best words I have ever heard," solemnly replied the prisoner.[14]

Employment was one of the conditions of parole, and among the records of the Court of Pardons is a form letter signed by one of Titus' long-standing friends, Thomas B. Howell ("Business: Caterer and restaurateur") promising him a job. However Titus, a model prisoner, had become bookkeeper of the prison's shoe department, and had handled the business of one firm so well that an accounting position awaited him there.

On December 27, 1904, he bid the keeper and his assistants a tearful farewell, and started for home accompanied by two Hackettstown friends. Going out into the street, he stamped about for a full minute in the snow, "the first I've touched in nineteen years," he said,[15] after which the trio walked all the way down to the State House, where Lizzie was waiting for him. They reached Hackettstown after 10 that evening. Titus' mother and friends had a small party to welcome him back to the house on Sharp Street, where he lived until June 1952 without ever again speaking of the events that cost him so many years of his life.

Chapter Eight

What follows is not history but analysis, as we examine the cases for and against James Titus. That the evidence against him was circumstantial is a matter of documented fact, but circumstance can hang a suspect as well as a "smoking gun" when made to appear as compelling. The state's objectives were to establish that Titus alone had the motive and the opportunity to commit the crime, and that his actions before and after the crime were evidence, respectively, of premeditation and guilt.

It accomplished both. The prosecutors, two very capable attorneys, overcame the lack of hard evidence by hammering the odd circumstances into an apparently strong chain. Whether each individual link was strong and the chain as faultless as it appeared is what we will now consider, although in retrospect it seems to have made little difference at the time: 12 men in a jury box were convinced that it was, and that was the bottom line. It remains now for the reader to decide whether the abstraction we call justice can be an integral part of an equation whose terms include smoke and mirrors.

State v. James J. Titus was no simple case of there being only two possibilities: A and B, and if not A therefore B. In the absence of hard evidence, the prosecutors had to prove their case as if they were determining the shapes of missing pieces in a jigsaw puzzle by the shapes of the adjacent pieces.

But a real jigsaw puzzle has a picture and colors to aid in the process. The Titus case, by contrast, was a monochromatic puzzle with no picture at all, one in which several different pieces might seem to fit a given space without a clue as to which was the "right" one.

Each argument the state could put forth to establish Titus' guilt was susceptible to being blunted by an equally plausible alternative from the defense, for in the end it all came down to suppositions. Given this situation the prosecutors' success in obtaining a conviction is less amazing than the defense attorneys' inability to persuade the jury that some degree of reasonable doubt existed.

Perhaps the emotional force of the crime and the need to call someone to account for it proved in the end more persuasive than either side's arguments.

A careful reading of the trial transcript supports the argument that Titus' guilt was never established beyond reasonable doubt. The state never proved that rape had been committed at the time and place alleged, let alone that Titus had committed it.

Consider this.

"Man's lust is a potent force," Prosecutor Henry S. Harris declared in the opening of a summation that went on to accuse Titus of sacrificing the life of Tillie Smith to it. Indeed lust is a potent force, but was the state's position credible that Titus' lustful thoughts, evidenced by allegedly salacious remarks to Mead and others, foretold criminal activity? How many millions have made passing remarks of the same type and never followed them with an antisocial act? What minister has not had less-than-religious thoughts about a parishioner; what accountant has not considered embezzlement? Who can argue reasonably that the thought being the father of the deed extends, as a general rule, to crime?

William Van Syckle testified about Titus' lewd remarks. George Thompson swore that Titus claimed he had his hand on Tillie Smith's leg more times than he had fingers, and Mead that Titus had described Tillie Smith to him as "the kind of girl one might have a racket with" (which is to say one of easy virtue). But if language that is lewd, but not in itself illegal, proves anything at all it may be only that the speaker has a so-called dirty mind, not that he will commit rape and murder.

Mead swore that on the night of the crime Titus had told him Tillie was coming in late, and that Mead could join him in "pumping" her. If the word Titus allegedly used meant what Mead thought it did, are we to assume this man of supposedly lewd disposition was reluctant to use the equivalent, less obscure four-letter Anglo-Saxon term in order to spare the budding clergyman's sensibilities, even while asking him to join in the act?

Did the word actually have the meaning that Mead understood it to have, or was it Mead who had the lewd disposition? J.G. Shipman asked this question in his summation rhetorically.

We will never know. This was all the prosecutors could submit as evidence of Titus' state of mind. It offers precious little to support their contention that on the night of April 8, unable to control his lust any longer, he had accosted poor virginal Tillie as she reentered the Institute, had been rebuffed by her, and had murdered her while accomplishing his purpose by force.

Accepting the state's contentions also requires that we ignore Titus' personal history. Defense counsel J.G. Shipman observed in his summation that "(m)en do not jump from virtue to crime at one single leap." To this one might add parenthetically, neither do they plan a felony for a little past 10 p.m. and invite the plumber in for a conference at 8:30, ask a minister-in-training to join in, and commit the act in a place where a couple of hundred people might overhear it.

If this is an accurate assessment of human behavior we must be cautious about accepting at face value what the state would have us believe. Is it reasonable to suppose that an intelligent and hitherto law-abiding man with an unblemished record, highly regarded in his community, completely trusted by his employer, a man without even a single complaint against him in 11 years of employment around female students and staff, can become a reckless, murderous rapist without warning, virtually overnight?

Such a change of character, while perhaps not totally impossible, is so unlikely that it warrants better proof than the state offered. Yet the state never once alleged that Titus had a history of criminal behavior, prior dalliances, insanity, public lewdness or drunkenness, nor did it offer evidence that his reputation in the community was anything but excellent.

While *The New York Times* of April 30, 1886, reported that "those in charge of the case" claimed to have received voluntary reports of Titus' bad conduct with female help at the Institute, the prosecution did nothing to develop those allegations, and no further mention of them was made. It seems unlikely, indeed preposterous, that such reports were dreamed up by *The Times*. Since "those in charge" did not disavow the reports, it seems likely that they invented them to weaken the defendant's standing in the public's mind and help strengthen their case. We can be sure that had Sylvester Smith possessed such damaging evidence he would have used it at trial. In the end, we are left with only a few idle conversations as the entire body of hard evidence about the defendant's moral disposition and state of mind. It is difficult to understand, given the quality of the evidence, how the allegation that the defendant was a debaucher could survive the test of reasonableness before a jury.

In establishing premeditation, the state relied not only on the testimony of Peter Mead, but on that of Niels Madsen, Titus' other student helper. The janitor's going up to Madsen's room to tell him that he didn't need to come down unless he wanted to, was offered as proof that he intended to keep the young Dane out of the basement in order to guarantee privacy with Tillie that night.

But how private a setting could he have desired if he was willing to have Mead join him in "pumping" her? His remark to Madsen, that he didn't have to come down unless he felt like, was hardly a directive to stay away. As if that weren't enough, Madsen was unable to remember whether Titus had made that remark on Thursday, April 8, or Wednesday, April 7. If it was made on the Wednesday, Titus couldn't possibly have made it for premeditative purposes, since Tillie didn't tell him of her plan to return late until supper time on Thursday. And while the state argued that Titus made a special trip upstairs to Madsen's room for that purpose, Madsen himself testified that the janitor had been cleaning in the vicinity of his room and had stopped in to speak with him because it was convenient.

When we consider all the related testimony, it seems reasonable to believe that Madsen's help really wasn't needed on the evening of April 8. Recall that Dr. Whitney testified that the steam boilers were not in use that time of year, although the furnace was kept fired up for hot water. Would there have been enough demand for coal to require Madsen's help? Recall, too, that Mead had left the basement that night after spending only about 20 minutes, mostly in conversation, so that he could study for a history examination.

Thus, even if Titus had ordered Madsen outright not to come down that evening, it would have been understandable; there wasn't enough work to keep Mead busy either.

With respect to Mead's testimony in general, we see that much of it was based on notes about "incriminating" conversations with Titus beginning shortly after the reward was announced.

We should probably begin by asking ourselves, as the defense asked Mead, why he was keeping notes of the conversations at all, since his explanation was barely credible. Throughout his cross-examination by Mercer Beasley, Mead repeatedly denied that he kept notes to prove his role in Titus' arrest and conviction so that he could claim the $1,000 reward. He was adamant in his denials, yet on June 13, 1887, he wrote to the Hackettstown Council:

> As there has been a reward of $1,000 Dollars offered to any person or persons who would give evidence that would lead to the conviction of the murderer of Matilda Smith who was killed on April 8th 1886 I Peter F. Mead of said place being the person who gave the evidence which convicted the murderer of said Matilda Smith claim said reward or part there of as your honorable body deem I justly deserve.

The jury may have been unable to see this side of Mead's character during the trial, but with the benefit of hindsight we are certainly entitled to speculate about the man's integrity. What can we say about a ministerial student who claims to be another's friend, encourages him to talk, swears convincingly that he has no interest at all in a reward, and then lays claim to it when his testimony nearly places that friend's neck in a noose?

That he was a liar? Treacherous? Perhaps even these descriptions are too kind. Mead appears to have been the only person at the Institute with whom Titus conversed at any length or shared any confidences. If the janitor was guilty of anything, it may well have been poor judgment in his choice of friends.

There is no evidence that anything but a casual acquaintanceship existed between the two men. Except for Mead's allegations, there is no evidence that Titus' side of the relationship was ever anything more than business-like. There is certainly no indication that it ever developed to a level at which the older man would suggest they share a sexual partner and expect to be taken seriously. The two were not "drinking buddies" nor did they socialize during nonworking hours.

Because Titus chose not to take the stand and the alleged conversations with Mead were held in private we, like the jury, have only Mead's accounts of them. But even if we give Mead the benefit of the doubt, even if we concede for argument's sake that his accounts of the alleged conversations in the basement and around the grounds were totally accurate and complete, just how useful are they in establishing prior intent or later guilt?

No testimony was elicited from him about the context in which the supposedly suggestive conversations about Tillie occurred. Have we any reason to believe that Titus was serious about Mead joining him in "pumping" Tillie? Would a reasonable man suddenly invite a casual acquaintance, a seminarian, to join him in committing a major indiscretion — possibly a felony?

Couldn't he have been joking? Mead's "Oh, pshaw!," a statement of mildly irritated disbelief, is the equivalent of today's "Awwww, come on," and seems less an expression of repulsion at the janitor's remark than one of annoyance at an obvious put-on.

Recalling the picture of Mead which emerges from his testimony, we see more a self-important prig than a humble seminarian; a man who styled himself "Reverend" even though he was still a student; a witness who attempted to show his superiority by playing word games with attorney Beasley. Given Mead's personality, Titus' sexual innuendoes may well have been more an attempt to tease him than disclose his intentions.

Similarly, Titus' questions both to Mead and Matron Ruckle about whether God could forgive the perpetrator of such a crime, might just as well have been an ironic comment on religion from a church dropout as a question about his own chances of salvation.

Mead's records of his own conversations with Titus were limited and shamelessly selective. The statements of Titus that he recalled best, and which were alleged to be the most incriminating, were related in considerable detail but not always in context. For example, Mead testified on direct examination that on the night of the murder he went to the basement, that he and Titus began talking as soon as he arrived there, and that they continued talking until the plumbers arrived, about 20 minutes in all. Yet, despite his extraordinary memory of other conversations, all Mead could recall of that 20 minutes was the single remark about "pumping" Tillie, and his own excuse about having to study.

There was no reference to any conversation which might have preceded or followed those subjects, no reference to standing around the sink with Titus and William Drake as the plumber demonstrated his working model.

Even if we concede, again for purposes of argument, that the state succeeded in establishing Titus' state of mind beyond reasonable doubt, we must still ask whether it also proved that he had a clear opportunity to do something about it.

Even if Titus' conversation with Mead and the others established unquestionably that he planned to have sexual relations with Tillie Smith that very night, the state still needed to place him at the scene of the crime. This was problematic at best — by the state's own reckoning, only a single, narrow window of opportunity existed. That window opened at about 10:15 p.m., since the fact of Tillie's arrival on the Institute grounds at 10:10 p.m. could not be disputed, and it closed when the defendant allegedly met his victim just inside the cellar door less than 10 minutes later. Unexpected repairs to a bedstead had caused Titus to run slightly behind his usual schedule that night, and as a result he rang the lights-out bell later than usual.

He had thrown the front door bolt at 10:10 p.m., a time verified by Munnich, who was standing only a few yards away on the front walk. If Tillie and Munnich spent another four or five minutes saying their good-byes, and if the walk from just inside the front gate to the rear entrance consumed an additional minute or two, Tillie would have been at the laundry room entrance at 10:16 — perhaps 10:17 at the latest. Had she not told Munnich she was headed directly there? It follows that she would have had to be accosted by Titus on entering the basement at that time, plus or minus a minute or two at most. Indeed, it would have been necessary for Titus to strangle her then and there to commit the rape in the manner described by the prosecution.

So vital was this time element to the state's case that both prosecutors reiterated it during their summations. First, Smith:

> He doubtless was there, or would be there, waiting for her; he would then become familiar and more familiar until there became a struggle.

Then Harris:

> It was 10:10. She left him (Munnich) declaring her intention of going to the laundry door, where Titus was. They must have met there. There is a discrepancy of a minute in the time when she was to get there and when he got there...He said he was awake all night and went around the building at 10:15. Munnich and Tillie stayed there three or four minutes after the lights went out, and the girl started to go. Mr. Titus *must* have met the girl at that door and seen her as she came in. That door was probably locked that night. He *had* to let her in. [emphasis added]

But where would Titus have been at the time? Recalling Dr. Whitney's description of his duties, the janitor would have been working his way through the enormous building checking that gaslights were turned down and windows shut. There was no evidence offered that he had not made his full rounds after bolting the front door, nor was he seen tearing through the Institute at superhuman speed (as he would have to have done) so that he could return to the basement in time to meet Tillie at the door. There could be no expectation that she would return at a particular time, or even at all, unless Titus' inquest testimony about Tillie's threat to stay out all night was a complete fabrication.

Furthermore, the prosecution arguments were mutually exclusive: Either the door was locked, and Titus had to let Tillie in, or it was open, in which case she either was accosted as she entered or lingered in the furnace room until the janitor returned. Which was it? Surprisingly, the defense failed to dispute the state on one of the most fundamental assumptions of its case: the conjectured opportunity to commit the crime.

But even if Titus had accomplished the near-impossible and had reached the cellar just in time to intercept the hapless Tillie, the state's case contained still other flaws.

First, there was the matter of establishing that rape had been committed. Its commission was *inferred* from the discovery of both sexual intercourse and strangulation, but there was absolutely no compelling medical evidence (such as indications of forcible penetration) to establish a better relationship between the two.

It might be argued that this simply begs the question and that the victim should receive the benefit of the doubt. But this was a real case with a real defendant and a real gallows looming large at the end of it. Rape was the single aggravating factor that brought the case within the scope of a statute that subjected the defendant to the death penalty. When life is at stake, overly broad inferences can't suffice. Justice Beasley made that point in his charge to the jury, when he reminded them that "[i]nferences in a case like this ought to be founded on facts thoroughly proven — thoroughly proven." Were the state's inferences thoroughly proven?

When the body was first discovered the *Washington Star* reported that "[t]he theory generally accepted was that the girl had been brutally outraged and murdered..." This was a conclusion understandably reached by laymen. But could a group of medical examiners reach the same conclusion when their own autopsy records and observations didn't support it? Might it have been their Victorian sensibilities that refused to acknowledge the possibility that a female employee of a Methodist seminary could be anything less than spotlessly virtuous? Was it, perhaps, the paradigm of human behavior in that time and place that made it unimaginable that a young single female's sexual intercourse and subsequent murder could *not* be related?

This leads us to J.G. Shipman's insinuations concerning

Tillie's prior chastity, which may, under the circumstances, be seen as having had some purpose other than defaming the victim's character.

Contemporary readers may be offended by the introduction of such evidence in a rape trial; it is excluded in today's courtrooms. That said, it must be remembered that we are dealing with a 19th-century case in which the court considered it not only proper but also important.

Justice Beasley addressed this point during the examinations of Sherer, Dolan and Gray, and near the start of his charge to the jury remarked:

> (T)he evidence as to the character of the girl is legitimate evidence, for a rape has been charged. It is important in a case of this kind. I don't know its bearing, but it may raise a presumption that she went off with some other person.

Mercer Beasley raised this possibility in his summation when he spoke of the missing hairpins, gloves and purse:

> (S)uppose she had met someone — a former lover — who was jealous, and he had joined her and they had walked off. She might have given them to him and after that the difficulty might have occurred. She might have gone off with someone she knew — not a stranger.

Besides raising a reasonable doubt about rape, the strategy had an additional advantage: If the victim were shown to be a person to whom sexual activity was customary, then the prosecution's highly emotional appeal, avenging the outrage of an innocent virgin who died defending her honor, would be blunted. In so circumstantial a case, the possibility of consensual sexual intercourse followed by a possibly unrelated robbery and murder deserved at least as much consideration as the possibility of murder committed during rape. The defense's attempt to call the character of the victim into question, then, was understandably prudent given the accepted practices of the day. One wonders whether Beasley's reference to "a former lover" was specifically to Frank Weeder, who had been in the area and made contact with her on the night of the murder but escaped becoming a serious suspect.

There is also the question of whether the state proved beyond a reasonable doubt that the crime was committed in the Institute basement, and not somewhere nearer the place where the body was found. Frank, the Pinkerton detective, concluded from his investigation that the crime had occurred in the Stewart barn, where he claimed to have discovered signs of a struggle. Dr. Cook testified at the inquest that he had examined that same barn, and that in his opinion the dust and dirt in the victim's hair and clothing were similar to some that he saw there. The inquest agreed.

But even if Stewart's barn had not been the murder site, there were other outbuildings with similar environments nearby, including the Institute's own stable. It was not until a trio of New York reporters became involved in the investigation that the detectives' attention was directed away from outbuildings and toward the Institute.

How reasonable was that change of direction? More than 150 people were in the Institute building at 10:15 p.m., many of them still awake. Some had their windows partly open and others were lying in beds only a few feet above the same cellar that Prosecutor Harris claimed was the site of shrieks, screams and a life-and-death struggle. Does it seem likely under those circumstances that no one in the building would hear a sound?

But there is more. To move the body from the Institute to the spot at which it was found, Titus would have had to drag and/or carry a dead weight greater than his own directly beneath windows from which he could have been easily observed, for more than 400 feet. The weather was clear and cold, and although the moon had set by 10 o'clock some students at their windows after lights-out could see. Yet no one saw anything unusual.

One could easily imagine that Titus, a man with some experience moving loads, might have used one of the coal wheelbarrows to transport the body quickly and quietly, but the complete absence of coal dust in the victim's clothing eliminated that possibility.

No, said the state: He half-carried, half-dragged the body for 400 feet in plain view of the residents as he passed beneath their windows. He even carried it past two deep cesspools with whose locations he was totally familiar, whose covers were easily removed, and in which the body could have been concealed with no chance of discovery. It seems beyond comprehension that, after his cool behavior in the basement, he would fail to dump the body in either, but chose instead to carry it still further to an open field in which it would be easily seen.

What did Titus' appearance and behavior in the days following the crime prove? He seemed nervous and upset, consulted with a lawyer, read his Bible because he felt he was "in trouble," allegedly asked Mead about the inquest, and indicated that he could use an alibi. He made remarks about forgiveness, had never gone to see Tillie's body, and apparently didn't proclaim his innocence loudly enough to please his critics. Mead allegedly saw him examining certain basement windows from the outside. He ordered the drying room floor swept, contrary to Dr. Whitney's opinion that it did not need sweeping. He asked a postal clerk about how they treated prisoners in state prison.

But, with a swarm of New York reporters descending on Hackettstown, and the finger of suspicion pointed at him daily, wouldn't Titus, or anyone else for that matter, have been nervous, upset and troubled?

What person in that position wouldn't want to examine what the daily press insisted was the evidence of his crime. Wouldn't any reasonable person consult a lawyer if he felt he was under suspicion of murder? No one ever said that Titus was a fool.

But there was something else, a flaw so fundamental that had it been revealed the case would never have reached the jury. Justice Beasley's charge pointed up the importance of determining where the parties were at various times on the night of April 8, concentrating on the window of opportunity between 10:10 p.m. and 10:20 p.m., alleged to be the only time at which the crime could have been committed. Overlooked by all was a blatant discrepancy between the charges set forth in the indictment and the evidence of three of the state's principal witnesses, Coroner Jesse Smith and doctors John S. and Richard Cook.

The doctors had estimated their arrival at the field where Tillie's body lay as between 9:30 and 10 a.m. They further estimated that the victim had been dead six or seven hours *at that time,* possibly since midnight. The inquest placed the time of death *pro forma* between April 8 at about 10:15 p.m., when Tillie was last seen alive, and April 9 at 8:45 a.m., when White discovered her body. The Cooks' examinations in the field and during the autopsy were sufficiently compelling that Coroner Smith completed and signed a death certificate establishing the date of death as April 9. Two doctors and a coroner, all three of them the state's own experts, testified that the victim died on that date, and the death certificate that issued attested to their professional opinions.

Of what value, then, was the window of opportunity that opened for only half an hour on the previous night? Because that window was so painstakingly designed and constructed by prosecutors Smith and Harris, it absolutely precluded commission of the crime at any other time than April 8 between 10:15 and 10:30 p.m.

The death certificate could have brought the state's entire case crashing down. The indictment on which Titus was brought to trial alleged in each and every one of its three counts both that the defendant committed each offense, and that the victim had died on April 8. It is astounding, in view of the degree to which timing was so crucial to the prosecution's case, that so obvious a discrepancy could be overlooked. But the death certificate was never entered in evidence, nor is there any indication that the Shipmans ever saw it. Let alone contested it!

Was its significance simply missed by everyone involved in the case? Unlikely. Any capable defense attorney who saw the death certificate would have realized its significance, and would have demanded a dismissal of all the charges once the state rested, instead of bothering to mount a defense. Titus would have walked out of the courtroom a free man.

Was the document suppressed once the prosecutors realized its implications? Such tactics are not unheard of, and in this instance seem all the more likely given the public pressure to solve the crime.

Summing up, the accused denied repeatedly that he committed the crime, no one either saw or heard him commit it, and the state failed to prove that it was committed in the place it contended, and at the date and time alleged in the indictment.

The state alleged that Titus' statements about Tillie prior to her death established motive, yet none of the evidence it presented was compelling. All of Mead's testimony, given his later actions, seems tainted, and Titus' alleged remark about "pumping" Tillie, had it been made at all, might have simply been made in jest.

No one had seen Tillie near the basement door, let alone entering the basement that night. While Munnich had sworn she told him she was locked out and would have to enter by the laundry door, and Arturo Rivera and Harry Smith had watched her until she disappeared from view, her entering the building remained pure conjecture.

There was also a lack of unequivocal physical evidence of rape, and much of the forensic evidence was explainable in ways helpful to the defense. For example, the quantity of semen recovered from the body suggested that the victim might have had intercourse with two men that night, supporting an earlier argument that two men would have been required to commit the crime because of Tillie's considerable physical strength.

The absence of semen stains on the undergarments suggests that the body, if carried, would have been carried horizontally, a near-impossibility for one person.

There were bruises on the *sides* of Tillie's head that were consistent with blows, but not with the prosecution's assertion that her hair had become undone because the *back* of her head had been repeatedly banged on the floor during an assault.

The splinters and dust in her clothing could just as easily have come from Shield's Hall, Stewart's barn, the Institute's stables or King & Bowlby's workroom as from the Institute's basement. The state offered floor boards from the Institute as evidence to show that the fibers in Tillie's clothing were the same as those from the boards. They may have been "the same as," but the microscope expert Dr. Oseler was unprepared to swear what type of tree the splinters came from, and certainly not that they came from those very same boards to the exclusion of all others.

It will be recalled that when the body was discovered there had been a board lying across its outstretched arm — a sturdy hemlock plank too short to fit the nearby fence. This could have been the source of the "coniferous splinters" removed from the victim's dress. Suppose that plank had been used as a litter to carry the body.

Was justice done? No one will ever know the full story of what happened that April night more than a century ago, but this seems certain: Despite the web of circumstantial evidence, despite the peculiarities of his actions after the body was discovered, James Titus could not have murdered Tillie Smith as charged.

Even the affidavit, the so-called "confession," is suspicious. On every other occasion except that one he protested his innocence consistently, even vehemently. The very day before the affidavit was signed he restated it to his wife and mother. It is difficult to imagine him so talented an actor that he could bring tears to the eyes of spectators and win the admiration of a *Times* reporter with his pre-sentence speech. Why, after so many months of denial, would he suddenly confess his guilt — except that it was the last chance of saving his life? Can anyone seriously argue the alternative: that it would have been better, nobler, had he gone to the gallows protesting his innocence?

We will never know what happened. If Titus had any secrets to disclose, he took them to his grave in 1952, for all we have about the affair in his own words is the affidavit of March 1887 — the piece of paper with which the Shipmans saved his neck.

Chapter Nine

It is impossible to study a case such as this without suggesting other scenarios than the prosecution's that fit the evidence. A number of possibilities exist, and the reader will probably enjoy playing them out. The author's own choice follows, and
presents a theory that has as much hard evidence to substantiate
it as that on which Titus' prosecution was based.

There is some material to reconsider and some questions to
ask. The forensic testimony about the quantity of semen recovered from Tillie Smith suggested that two men were involved, her
known strength contributed to that view since it was supposed
that it would have required two men to overcome her.

The doctors Cook testified, and the death certificate indicated, that death occurred after midnight on April 9, not on April 8.

Tillie weighed 145 pounds, or about 10 pounds more than
James Titus, but we will suppose (for purposes of discussion) that
even in a weakened state he was somehow able to carry her dead
weight for more than 400 feet all by himself.

First, however, we must ask how the body might have been
carried quickly and quietly for that distance and what might have
resulted from its transit. This question was addressed during direct examination of Dr. Comegys Paul by the defense, and is of
particular significance. The matter under discussion was this:
Since all the semen found in the victim was located in the upper
region of the vagina near the mouth of the womb, why did it not
change position when the body was carried? The court seems to
have picked up the defense's line of reasoning immediately:

Q. (By the Court). You have stated that if the person, the woman
   whose vagina was filled with this semen had walked, it would
   have discharged itself, I understand?
A. No, sir; I did not say that.
Q. You said it would gravitate?
A. Now if a person with this substance in that location should get

up and walk, why of course that substance would gravitate downward towards the vulva.

Q. That is what I understood. Suppose the person were to be dragged any distance what would be the effect then upon the substance?

A. Dragged by the shoulders with the feet — lifted by the shoulders?

Q. Well, you may describe the different modes of dragging?

A. Well, your Honor, it depends of course altogether on the position of this part of the body (indicating the hips). If the body was taken by the shoulders and dragged, of course that would allow this part of the body to be lower, and therefore it would gravitate.

Q. The semen would not be found in the position described?

A. It would not be found up by the womb.

Q. If the body were carried up in the arms?

A. Then, if the body were carried with the shoulders resting so on one arm, and the knees on the other, of course that would leave the hips lower and then it would gravitate in the same way.

Q. Then your idea is that if the body were carried so, up a pair of stairs, the head being raised and the lower part of the body in the position in which a person would naturally carry a body then the semen would dislodge itself from the place and be lower down?

A. It would. It would slide down towards the external organ.

Q. It would not be up as high as it was described to you in the question?

A. It would not...[1]

The examination continued with the various ways in which a body might be carried, but the results were always the same: Lowering the hips meant shifting the vaginal contents to a lower position, regardless of whether a person was dead or alive. On cross-examination by Henry Harris, the one remaining possibility was put forth:

Q. If the body was carried without elevating the shoulders, then it would be in the condition described, it would not gravitate?

A. That would not be likely to gravitate from the location in which it was, unless the hips of the individual were lowered, of course, if it laid in a horizontal position, it would not be likely to change its place. It would not be so likely, it might.

Q. If carried in any way so that the hips were not lowered, it would still remain there?

A. Well, you will understand that that is more a question of mathematics. If that discharge is here while the body is lying in a horizontal position, any change of that position so that there would be an inclination downwards, would have an influence in making it gravitate.

Q. But no motion that kept it in a horizontal position or only elevated the feet would have that effect?

A. I cannot imagine how anybody could be carried that way.

Q. *I didn't ask you that question.* [emphasis added][2]

One imagines that Harris' last remark was made with a note of alarm. It was established that Titus didn't use one of the wheelbarrows to carry the body, because there were no traces of coal dust in the clothing. The most likely way he could have accomplished the task would be to balance the body over his shoulder with its head down and to the rear, his arms wrapped around the legs just below the knees in a so-called "fireman's carry."

He might also have grasped it under the arms and, walking backward, dragged it along with its heels scraping the ground. He might even have alternated between the two.

But no matter which method he could reasonably have used, the effects of jostling, of gravity, and of the body's lack of muscle tone would have caused leakage of the vaginal contents.

It will be recalled, too, that even though the body was fully dressed and the autopsy physicians found copious amounts of semen, not a trace of it was found on the undergarments.

The alternative proposed by Smith, that the body might have been carried in Titus' arms in a more or less horizontal position for the entire distance seems preposterous, especially when the carrier is outweighed by the victim. But two people could have carried Tillie's body in a horizontal position quite easily, simply by placing it on a sturdy board — say, a rough-sawed pine or hemlock board such as one might find lying around a barn or stable.

It was mentioned earlier that Frank Weeder, Tillie's former boyfriend, seems to have received a much more cursory examination by the authorities than conditions warranted. This conclusion is based on inconsistencies between statements Weeder and his friend Charles Huff made at the inquest, and those Weeder made to *The World* a short time later.

First, he had testified at the inquest that after the show at Shield's Hall he had seen Tillie, the Wright sisters and Annie Van Syckle on the "post office corner," which is to say Main and Church streets.

He had also testified that he was with Jesse Baggot when he called Mary Wright to one side, with the object of getting the women to leave the strangers' company. Afterward, he said, he had left Baggot and joined his other friends — Hann, Tineman and Search — and that all four had gone to Tineman's grocery, where they drank cider. Finally, they had all gone back uptown at about 12:30 a.m., and he had seen nothing more of the strangers or the women after having left the post office corner.

But when Weeder spoke with *The World*, his account of the evening had changed significantly. Now, he told for the first time how he had whistled to Tillie when she was with Munnich, and how he had been in the group that lit matches in Harry Haring's and Annie's Van Syckle's faces.

But Huff had sworn at the inquest that the match-lighters who accompanied him were Keggan, McWilliams and Johnston. He had made no mention at all of Weeder being with them.

Since the match-lighting incident had occurred nearly half an hour after Weeder whistled to Tillie and spoke with her, he must either have lied to the inquest about having left the post office corner, gone to Tineman's, and seen nothing more of the women or the strangers afterward; lied to *The World's* reporter about being with the match-lighters; or lied to both.

Let's explore these possibilities further. On direct examination by Prosecutor Smith, Mary Wright made only the most oblique reference to a conversation with Weeder at the post office corner on the evening of the murder:

Q. State what occurred after all of you stopped there? (in front of the Methodist Church)

A. We stood and talked a few minutes and I excused myself to Miss Smith and excused myself to Mr. Weeder.

Q. Who is Mr. Weeder?

A. Mr. Frank Weeder.[3]

So, we know he was on the scene at a few minutes before 10, although initially not in front of the post office (or "on the post office corner") as he had said, but on the opposite side of Main Street, in front of Trinity church.

George Search, the friend being sought by Mary Wright, was a member of Weeder's gang, as was Annie Van Syckle's regular boyfriend, Charles Lee; and Tillie Smith was Weeder's own ex-girlfriend. Consequently, Weeder's interest in the salesmen does not seem surprising.

A couple of minutes later, according to Munnich, when he and Tillie had entered Church Street — which would put them at the side of the post office building — two strangers whistled Tillie over and spoke with her briefly. He said she seemed to know them; since all of Munnich's other statements were verified, there is no reason to doubt this one.

It appears that after confronting Mary Wright in front of the church, ostensibly to warn her away from the strangers, Weeder and one of his friends crossed Main Street in order to intercept Tillie and Munnich next to the post office. Since Tillie had probably seen and heard Weeder warning Mary Wright away in front of the Methodist church, one can imagine that she was concerned to find herself accosted by him only seconds later.

Concerning his whereabouts after the whistling incident, Weeder told the inquest that immediately after talking with Mary Wright he left the post office corner and went with his friends (including George Search) to Tineman's to drink cider. He added that it was after midnight when he left his friends, and that he saw nothing further of the women or the strangers after leaving the corner.

Besides the obvious inconsistency of his going off drinking with a fellow he'd just told Mary Wright she had a date with, how could he have been one of the people who lit matches in Annie Van Syckle and Harry Haring's faces nearly half an hour later, as he told *The World*?

Did Weeder lie to the inquest concerning his whereabouts or to *The World* about being involved in the match-lighting incident? Or did he lie to both? He would certainly have benefited from concealing his activities on the night of the murder. He had only recently been jilted by Tillie, and would immediately have been labeled a suspect if it were known he had spoken to her barely 15 minutes before she was last seen alive and couldn't account for himself afterward.

It entailed some risk to admit speaking with Mary Wright in front of the church, but considerably less than trying to deny what she had already testified to, and still less than admitting to the inquest that he had spoken to Tillie in front of the post office. He would have been unable to swear at the inquest that he had hung around the corner of Main and Church streets afterward and was in the group of match-lighters, because Huff had testified only a few minutes before and had named all his companions.

Liable to become a suspect if he was known to be anywhere near the area of the crime at 10:30 p.m., and unable to claim having been with Huff and the others, it would have been advantageous for him to claim he was with his other friends Hann, Tineman and Search, that they had gone to Tineman's grocery and drank cider, and didn't come back uptown until after midnight.

Three weeks later, with the investigators' full attention focused on the seminary basement and the arrest of Titus a foregone conclusion, Weeder could admit to having spoken with Tillie. As a safety measure, he would divert further suspicion by claiming he participated in some minor mischief that had a verifiable time and place — match-lighting on the corner of Church and Main streets at 10:25 p.m. It was a small risk, but who would recall some minor points of testimony by an unimportant witness at a highly confidential inquest nearly three weeks earlier? Most people were too interested in Titus by then to care.

Which leaves us with this question: Where did Frank Weeder go after speaking with Tillie? Might he have left Huff and the match-lighters (which was why Huff couldn't place him at Church and Main streets at 10:25 p.m.), and gone somewhere else with another of his friends? Perhaps with George Search, who never did manage to meet Mary Wright that evening? Did they go, not to Tineman's for cider, but to another place far too dangerous to disclose to anyone?

Now that we have the pieces in place, let's play out this scenario and see what might have happened.

It is nearly 10 p.m. Tillie Smith and Charles Munnich have just crossed Main into Church Street for the walk to Centenary's front gate. In the darkness on Church Street, a few feet beyond the building line, Frank Weeder and George Search have been sharing a bottle of whiskey, and Frank's gotten curious — and perhaps a little angry — about Tillie's companion.

He and Tillie were going together until very recently, but his possessiveness and his gang friends troubled her, and she broke off the relationship. He is a jealous type, but cool-headed. After warning away Mary Wright, he crosses back to the post office and watches to see what Tillie will do next. As she and Munnich cross Main and enter Church Street, he whistles and calls softly to her. She recognizes his voice in the darkness and, leaving Munnich's side, walks a few yards to where he stands. Out of earshot of Munnich, she tells him to stop following her around, but he is disarmingly friendly and asks to see her again. Perhaps he tells her he's worried about the stranger and only wants to keep an eye on her to be sure she's safe. After a few seconds, they arrange to meet near one of the outbuildings at the rear of the seminary — perhaps Stewart's barn, perhaps Centenary's stable — after Munnich has dropped her off.

She returns to Munnich's side and the two continue walking toward the Institute. Weeder and his companion follow them quietly at a distance on the opposite side of Church Street, perhaps cutting over to Plane Street so that they will be completely out of sight. As Tillie and Munnich enter the Institute grounds, the two men reach the corner of Plane and Jefferson streets, and continue down Plane toward the rear of the Institute building.

Now it is 10:10 p.m. Tillie and Munnich are standing on the front walk talking, when they hear the loud click of the front door bolt as Titus engages it. Munnich notices lights starting to go out, checks his pocket watch and notes the time; meanwhile, Arturo Rivera and Harry Smith have been watching the couple from their dormer.

Tillie tells Munnich that she is locked out, and will have to go around to the basement entrance. They speak for another couple of minutes, then part. Munnich walks back through the main gate, crosses Jefferson, and begins walking up Church Street. Tillie, meanwhile, walks toward the front of the Institute, disappearing from Rivera and Smith's view as she draws closer to the building. Turning right, she steps onto the wooden walkway leading to the rear, and Munnich hears the echo of her footsteps as she disappears around the side of the building.

She reaches the stairway leading to the cellar entrance door, which Titus left unlocked in case she returned while he was making his rounds, but bypasses it. Instead, she cuts diagonally across the rear of the Institute grounds in the direction of Centenary's stable — where Frank is waiting, his friend standing off at a short distance.

As the temperature is continuing to drop, he suggests that they all go inside to keep warm.

The stable floor is dusty and littered with straw, coarse sawdust, splinters of wood and dry leaves. Tillie and her companions enter, and she spreads her cloak out on the floor to keep her dress and jacket from getting too dirty. Perhaps she and Frank Weeder huddle together against the cold. They talk, but as Weeder continues to drink, his mood begins to turn ugly. His conversation becomes accusatory, and he berates her about Munnich, tells her that she belongs only to him.

He attempts to embrace her, but Tillie is strong-willed and won't be told what to do. She protests, and pushes him away while trying to rise to her feet, but he slaps her roughly across the side of her head and tells her to shut up.

She falls backward, opening the partly healed cut on her left hand, and is momentarily stunned. Aroused by liquor, rage and the opportunity provided by the deserted setting, Weeder falls upon her. She is physically a fair match for him until his friend joins in and pulls her jacket down from behind, pinioning her arms. He holds her as Weeder assaults her.

Tillie kicks and bucks, scuffing her shoes and grinding dirt, sawdust and leaves into the folds of her dress, but is unable to free herself.

She tries to scream, and is struck again.

When he is finished with her, Weeder offers her to his friend.

After a while, Tillie lies semi-conscious on the barn floor and it begins to dawn on the men that they're in serious trouble. If she identifies them, prison will be the best they can hope for — more likely, a lynch mob.

Weeder is young, but he's also hardened and streetwise. His friend will never talk; he's an accomplice and would share his punishment.

What options remain? Tillie can identify him only if she's allowed to leave the barn alive. He makes his decision. Kneeling partly astride her, one knee on the ground and the other pressing against her chest, his weight forces the air from her lungs. His hands close around her throat.

Now the men have only one thought — to get away. But first they need to move the body out into the open, away from the scene of the crime. It will be discovered there in daylight, but there are other buildings around and, if they're careful, enough no one will be able to tell exactly where the crime was committed. The drummer she was seen with might even be suspected. Wouldn't that be a laugh?

She is too heavy for one person to carry without leaving a trail. Seeing a rough hemlock plank lying against the wall, they lay it alongside the body. It is the right length and seems strong enough. They strip the body of anything of value — the new kid gloves, the breast pin, the small red purse containing her money and the spool of thread — to give the victim the appearance of having been robbed.

Tillie's jacket has come partially off in the struggle, and being unable to maneuver the body well enough to put the garment back on her completely, they give up and leave one of her arms outside its sleeve-hole.

Finally, they roll the body onto the board. The lower part of the dress snags on the rough-sawed edge and splinters are caught up in the fabric.

They grasp the ends of the board and carry the body out to the decaying fence at the border of Moore Street. There they slide the board across the bottom rail at an angle, twisting it to roll the body onto the ground. As the body rolls off the plank, its feet cross, and one arm is flung outward from the torso by the momentum. The other arm, closer to the ground at the beginning of the roll, remains parallel to the torso, and so Tillie comes to rest at an angle to the fence. The rolling motion causes the bottom of her dress to wind slightly around her ankles, giving it the appearance of having been tucked under.

Although her muscles are totally relaxed, there has been no leakage of fluids onto her undergarments because she has remained in a horizontal position throughout.

The rough hemlock board is pitched over the fence and comes to rest across Tillie's outstretched arm.

The killers return to the stable to await the dawn, when they can move about town less conspicuously. Once back inside, there is no more drinking, no more camaraderie; they need to obliterate all evidence of their having been at the scene before the body is discovered.

They find a lantern to generate enough light for gathering up loose hairpins; a handful of straw is used to sweep down the dirt on the floor and remove the more obvious traces of a struggle. The sky is beginning to lighten as they check one last time to make sure all traces of their presence are removed. They open the door a crack to make certain all is clear.

The liquor bottle, still half full, is pitched into the neighboring field as they leave. Matron Elizabeth Ruckle, an early riser, sees them from her window at daybreak, strolling casually across the rear of the Institute grounds, arm in arm, toward the railroad station.

So there it is, just a theory, although we will never know for certain who killed Tillie Smith.

We can't know: Once the authorities focused their attention on James Titus all other lines of investigation were dropped; a century later, they have disappeared.

Ultimate responsibility for the direction in which the investigation turned belongs to the state of New Jersey, even if the whip that drove it was firmly in the hands of the New York press. The trial and conviction of Titus happened because a community was inflamed beyond endurance by sensational journalism. The repeatedly expressed concern that a particularly heinous crime was going unsolved, the thinly veiled suggestions that the victim's social class entitled her only to neglect, the characterization of the victim as meek, and of her death struggle as heroic — all of these themes were orchestrated into an enormous crescendo from which release was provided in the person of an unfortunate janitor, and his conviction for a crime he could not possibly have committed. We can be reasonably certain that, by the time he stood in the dock, the outcome of the case was assured. He had already been tried and convicted in the press, and had virtually no chance of an impartial trial.

Was the performance of Titus' counsel adequate? In some respects it was, yet they missed important opportunities to substantially weaken the state's case. When we consider the way in which matters were finally resolved, we are left with the idea that the "confession" served several good purposes, regardless of its probable fabrication. The life of an innocent man was saved. The murder was considered solved. There was expiation and there was closure.

With all appeals exhausted and a date with the hangman two weeks off, Titus apparently grasped at the remaining straw. Who among us would have acted differently?

Epilogue

The monument to chastity, in whose cause Tillie Smith is said to have sacrificed her life, has kept its lonely vigil at the summit of the only hill in Union Cemetery for more than a century, remaining the most prominent feature of the grounds' most prominent place.

The plots that surround it are all long since occupied. Hackettstown has grown and the peaceful quiet of the little country cemetery has vanished. The tall trees that bordered its entrance path are also gone, victims of blight and pollution, and bird songs compete with the rattle and roar of traffic on the busy highway just across the river.

In a small family plot a short distance down the slope, a stone bears the names of James J. Titus and the generations of his family. Its last member, his widowed granddaughter, resided in the family home on Sharp Street until her death early in 1998.

I interviewed her in her living room, she seated on her floral-patterned sofa and I in James Titus' sturdy wooden rocker, as she recalled the impact that her grandfather's conviction had on the family.

Her great-grandmother had never lost faith in her son's innocence. Her own mother had her doubts. She had taken her aside when she was a young girl and had told her the story of her grandfather's conviction and imprisonment and the family's disgrace, lest she hear it first in the school playground or on the street. The mother had herself been harassed at the town library by an individual claiming to be a relative of Tillie Smith's, as if she were somehow to blame.

Asked what she thought about the affair, the granddaughter said she didn't really know what to think. It was never, ever spoken of around the house. And, even though she and her grandfather were on close terms, she could never bring herself to ask him about it.

I am glad that she had an opportunity to read a draft manuscript of this book before she died.

On a hill barely a mile away from the Titus home, the coppery green dome of Centenary's Seay Hall towers above a neighborhood whose tranquility was once shattered by an act of unspeakable brutality.

The college has grown and prospered, and is co-educational once again after having been a women's junior college for many decades. Tillie Smith has become something of a mascot there, popular superstition being that her spirit roams its corridors, protecting female students. They, in turn, leave votive candles, small offerings of food, and little crosses made of string-tied twigs on the pedestal of her monument.

More than a century has passed since the murder was committed, since the trial was held, the verdict rendered and the penalty paid, and still justice remains to be done.

Justice still smolders like an ember among the ashes of the Tillie Smith case, a dying spark which might yet be blown to life — that might live, as Robert Browning suggested, if precious be the soul of man to man.

Endnotes

Appendix

Bibliography

Notes to the Text

Records of the coroner's inquest no longer exist. Citations reading "Inquest" refer to reports of testimony given at the coroner's inquest that appeared in the Hackettstown Gazette and the Warren Reporter on April 16, 1886.

Citations reading "Transcript..." refer to the original two-volume bound transcript of Titus' 1886 trial at the New Jersey State Library's Rare Books Collection in Trenton. A microfilm copy of that document is also available at the state library.

The transcript to which references are made is a composite document assembled from several distinct copies — some originals and carbons of varying clarity. In addition to seven missing pages, it contains several obvious sequential errors in page numbering; consequently, references are made to microfilm reader indices as well as to page numbers. For example, "Testimony of Elizabeth Ruckle (1-447/0947)" indicates that her testimony begins in volume one of the original bound copy, at indicated page 447, and approximately at index number 0947 on a microfilm reader whose counter has been set to zero at page 1 of the transcript. To locate the beginning of any witness' testimony on microfilm, please refer to the Index of Testimony in the Appendix.

Preface

[1] "The daily newspapers keep fanning the flames, and hardly a day elapses but that fresh fuel is added. *The Sun*, *World* and *Herald* just now are running a race, and the reporter who gets up the most sensational article is considered the best fellow." (*Washington Star*, May 6, 1886); "We believe our citizens have been influenced too much by the New York papers to take a fair and impartial view of the facts in the case..." (*Hackettstown Gazette*, April 30, 1886); "(p)ublic sentiment has been manufactured too fast and public sentiment has often outraged Justice." (*Gazette*, May 7, 1886). *The Sun* had boasted of its role in the investigation: "(t)he Prosecutor has been kind enough to say that credit is due *THE SUN* for its persistent investigation by which the improbabilities of all the other theories for accounting for the murder were clearly set forth, and the only one natural chain of facts which led straight to the institute threshold was suggested." (*The Sun*, Thursday, April 29, 1886, page 3, column 1).

[2] Some of the more sensational local crimes of the period include the Changewater murders (1843); the murder of his wife by Rev. Jacob Hardin (1859); the murder of the Ritter children by their father (1876); and the Ballenscher (1888) and Andrews (1893) murders, described in Dale. *The New York Times* of April 13, 1886, mentions that "fears are cropping up that (the Tillie Smith murder) may pass to the record of crime along with the Orange Mountain and other uncleared tragedies" (page 5, column 4).

[3] A sample of publications that covered the case includes *The New York Times*, *The World*, *The Telegram*, *The Herald*, *The Tribune*, *The Sun*, *National Police Gazette*, the Easton (Pa.) *Express*, and virtually all the weekly newspapers in Warren County, N.J.

4 For example, the interviews of the victim's former boyfriend, Frank Weeder, and her mother, in *The New York World* of April 26, 1886; Peter Mead's interview in *The Sun* of May 2, 1886, and *The Herald* of May 10, 1886; and reference in the *Washington Star* of May 6, 1886, to a telephone interview of Titus in jail by a *Herald* reporter. Tillie's mother was also visited by *The New York Times* (April 13, 1886, page 5, column 4).

5 *The New York Times*, Oct. 13, 1886 (page 3, column 1).

6 *The New York Times*, Oct. 16, 1886 (page 2, column 2).

7 *Washington Star*, Nov. 11, 1886.

Chapter One

1 The decade 1860-1870 appears to have been the only profitable period for the canal. After 1870, nearly 35 percent of its coal transportation business was lost to the Delaware Lackawanna & Western Railroad and in 1881 all of its iron ore transportation business was lost to the Central Railroad of New Jersey. See Lee: *Morris Canal — A Photographic History.*

2 Typical advertisements for Centenary Collegiate Institute appear in the *Washington Star* of Oct. 21, 1886, and the *Hackettstown Directory* of 1885. See building details in Woodall (page 55) and the *Annual Catalogue of the Centenary Collegiate Institute, 1896-1897* (page 46).

3 Details of Centenary's history and student life are found in Woodall and in Custard. Snell (volume 2) contains detailed information about Centenary's construction financing, interior arrangements and furnishings. Biographical information and pictures of Dr. George H. Whitney appear in Snell: *Portrait and Biographical Record of Hunterdon and Warren Counties, New Jersey* in the collection of the Warren County library, Belvidere, N.J., and the archives of Centenary College, Hackettstown, N.J.

4 The Hackettstown portion of the New Jersey Census of 1885 (page 12) enumerates residents of Centenary Collegiate Institute on lines 336-518, listing 183 out of a total population of 2,645, a ratio of 6.9 percent.

5 It was suggested that blame for the crime was being directed at the Institute by tavern owners ("the rum element") to discredit Centenary's prohibition-minded seminarians (*The World*, May 2, 1886, and May 7, 1886). For their part, the anti-Prohibitionists suggested that prominent Methodists were trying to downplay the crime because it involved their seminary (*The World*, April 28, 1886). Fear of Centenary's influence on liquor licensing in Hackettstown seems exaggerated in any case, given that most students were either males under the age of 21 or disenfranchised females.

6 Testimony of Charles Reese (Transcript, 1-92/0159).

7 The following data for Hackettstown were developed using Distant Suns Ver.2.0 b., an astronomical program for personal computers, at approximately 40°20'N, 75°30'W on April 8-9, 1886, Phase = 0.15; Moonrise 8:21 a.m.; Moonset 10:45 p.m.

8 The times of Tillie's departure from Centenary and her arrival at Beatty & Karr's dry goods store (downstairs from Shields Hall) are necessarily estimates. The distance from Centenary to Shield's Hall was measured by engineer Augustus Dellicker and found to be 2,350 feet. (Transcript, 1-8/0011).

The Merrymakers' performance began at about 8 p.m. and Tillie was on time for it. If she went directly to Beatty & Karr's, spent 10 or 15 minutes there (to browse, pick out her spool of thread and pay for it), and another five or six minutes to walk outside the store, climb the stairs to the fourth floor and find her seat, she would have had to arrive at the store around 7:40 p.m. Covering a distance of 2,350 feet at a normal pace, considering the impediments of 19th century women's clothing, probably required around 15 or 20 minutes, hence an estimate that she departed Centenary between 7:20 and 7:25 p.m..

[9] Report of Dr. Conover's testimony at the inquest (*Hackettstown Gazette*, April 16, 1886, page 3); see also *The New York Times*, April 13, 1886 (page 5, column 4) and *The World*, April 14, 1886.

[10] Typical are Dr. Whitney's testimony that Tillie "bore an excellent reputation" (Inquest); that "she had the full esteem and confidence of her employers" (*Warren Republican*, April 18, 1886); and that "(she) gave entire satisfaction (at Centenary) and was highly thought of by every one" (*The World*, April 11, 1886).

[11] The clothing was recorded during the autopsy. Testimony of Dr. Richard Cook (Transcript, 1-588/1191), and described by Coroner Jesse Smith (Transcript, 1-137/0240).

[12] Testimony of Stella Sliker (Transcript, 1-201/0354).

[13] *Warren Republican*, April 16, 1886 (Matilda Smith Murder).

[14] Testimony of James Titus (Inquest). See also testimony of Jesse Smith (Transcript, 1-979/1879).

[15] Testimony of George Whitney (Transcript, 1-396/0857).

[16] Testimony of James Titus (loc. cit.)

[17] Testimony of George Beatty (Transcript, 1-226/0398). *Hackettstown Gazette* of April 16, 1886 (page 3) reports Beatty testified at the inquest that Tillie was wearing buff kid gloves and that he had to put her change directly into her pocketbook (apparently the gloves were too tight to allow easy finger movement).

[18] Various times were given, including Munnich's "(b)etween 9 and 10 o'clock" (Transcript, 1-319/0557); Haring's "I'm not positive when the show let out; I think it was twenty minutes of ten" (Inquest); Haring's "I should judge about half past nine or twenty minutes to ten" (Transcript, 1-461/0798); and Agnes Wright's "between nine and half past nine" (Transcript, 1-270/0475).

[19] Written statement of Harry Haring (Inquest); testimony of Charles Munnich (Transcript, loc. cit.).

[20] Written statement of Haring (Inquest).

[21] Testimony of Charles Munnich (Transcript, loc. cit.). Testimony of Mary Wright (Transcript, 1-234/0412).

[22] Testimony of Mary Wright (Transcript, loc. cit.). The person who spoke to her was Frank Weeder, Tillie's ex-boyfriend.

[23] Testimony of Charles Munnich (Inquest). The walk from the Methodist Church to Centenary appears to have been interrupted only once, for a few seconds, when two strangers whistled to Tillie and she spoke with them. The portion of Munnich's testimony that would have covered the walk down Church Street and the encounter with Frank Weeder next to the post office

have been excised from the transcript. See also *Washington Star*, April 15, 1886.

[24] This coincides with Dr. Whitney's testimony that Titus had been making some repairs to a bedstead as lights-out time approached, and was running several minutes behind his usual 10 p.m. tour of the building. The relevant portion of the transcript (Vol. 1, pp. 486-489) is missing, but an extract of Whitney's testimony was obtained from *Warren Journal*.

[25] Written statement of Haring (Inquest).

[26] Testimony of Charles Munnich (Inquest and Transcript, loc. cit.); testimony of Isaac Baldwin (Transcript, 2-983/1886); *The World*, April 25, 1886.

[27] Testimony of Harry Haring (Transcript, loc. cit.).

[28] Testimony of Charles Munnich (Inquest and Transcript, loc. cit.); testimony of Harry Haring (Inquest and Transcript, loc. cit.). See also *The New York Times*, April 13, 1886 (page 5, column 4), and *The World*, April 22, 1886.

Chapter Two

[1] *Washington Star*, April 15, 1886.

[2] Ibid. See also Inquest and Transcript (1-58/0098).

[3] Testimony of Coroner Jesse Smith (Transcript, 1-137/0240); Testimony of Dr. John S. Cook (Transcript, 1-500/1039). Compare this to *The World's* account of the "large ugly bruise" on the victim's forehead and the condition of her clothing "which hung in shreds about her body." (*The World*, April 10, 1886).

[4] Testimony of Charles Reese (Transcript, 1-92/0159).

[5] *Washington Star*, April 15, 1886; *Hackettstown Gazette*, April 16, 1886.

[6] Ibid.

[7] Testimony of Dr. John S. Cook (Inquest; also Transcript, 1-500/1039).

[8] Ibid. at 1-504/1045.

[9] Ibid. at 1-507/1049.

[10] Ibid. at 1-508/1050.

[11] Ibid. at 1-509/1051.

[12] Ibid. at 1-513/1057.

[13] *The New York Times*, April 12, 1886 (page 5, column 5); *Hackettstown Gazette*, April 16, 1886 (page 3).

[14] *The New York Times*, April 10, 1886 (page 3, column 2).

[15] Testimony of Frank Weeder (Inquest).

[16] *The New York Times*, April 12, 1886 (page 5, column 5); *Washington Star*, April 15, 1886.

[17] *The World*, April 15, 1886; *Washington Star*, April 15, 1886.

[18] *The New York Times*, April 15, 1886 (page 1, column 3); *The World*, April 15, 1886; *Hackettstown Gazette*, April 16, 1886.

[19] Testimony of Arturo Rivera (Transcript, 1-393/0681); testimony of Harry Smith (Transcript, 1-420/0729).

[20] *Washington Star*, April 15, 1886; *The World*, April 11, 1886.

[21] *The World*, April 14, 1886; *Washington Star*, April 15, 1886; *Warren Republican*, April 16, 1886.

[22] *The New York Times*, April 15, 1886 (page 1, column 3); *Hackettstown*

Gazette, April 16, 1886.

[23] The petition to the Mayor and Common Council contained nearly 70 signatures. It is designated Document No. 5877.25.26 in the collection of the Hackettstown Historical Society.

[24] *Washington Star*, Dec. 29, 1904.

[25] *The World*, April 21, 1886.

[26] Ibid., April 22, 1886.

[27] *Washington Star*, April 22, 1886.

[28] *Warren Republican*, April 23, 1886.

[29] *Belvidere Apollo*, April 23, 1886.

[30] *The World*, April 23, 1886.

[31] Ibid., April 24, 1886.

[32] *The World*, April 25, 1886.

[33] *Washington Star*, April 29, 1886.

[34] *Warren Republican*, May 7, 1886.

[35] *Warren Republican*, May 14, 1886.

[36] *The World*, April 29, 1886.

[37] *The World*, May 7, 1886

[38] *Hackettstown Gazette*, April 30, 1886.

[39] *Warren Republican*, May 14, 1886.

[40] *Hackettstown Gazette*, April 30, 1886.

[41] For example, *The World*: "the poor girl" (April 25, 1886); "a little country girl" (April 28); "little Tillie Smith" (April 30 and May 7).

[42] *The World*, April 29, 1886.

[43] *Hackettstown Gazette*, April 30, 1886.

[44] *Washington Star*, May 27, 1886.

Chapter Three

[1] Accounts of the arrest appear in the *Washington Star* (April 29, 1886), *The World* (April 29 and 30, 1886), *The New York Times* (April 29, 1886), *Hackettstown Gazette* (April 30, 1886) and *Warren Republican* (April 30, 1886).

[2] *The New York Times*, April 30, 1886 (page 1, column 4).

[3] *The World*, May 2, 1886.

[4] Woodall, op.cit.

[5] *Hackettstown Gazette*, May 7, 1886.

[6] Testimony of Peter Mead (Transcript, 1-754/1479).

[7] *Hackettstown Gazette*, May 7, 1886.

[8] *The Express* (May 8, 1886).

[9] *The New York Times*, May 9, 1886 (page 14, column 2).

[10] Ibid. See also *Hackettstown Gazette* (May 7, 1886) in which Mead is described as "the student who made the sworn statement upon which James J. Titus was arrested."

[11] Testimony of Peter Mead (Transcript, loc. cit.).

[12] To avoid confusion in the narrative, the name "Mercer Beasley" is used to denote the defense attorney; his father, identically named, is designated "Justice Beasley;" J.G. Shipman, formerly Judge of the Court of Chancery and known in some accounts as "Judge Shipman," is not referred to here by his title.

13 Testimony of Dr. J. M. Paul (Transcript, 2-1170/2213).

14 *Washington Star*, Sept. 30, 1886.

Chapter Four

1 *The New York Times*, Sept. 29, 1886 (page 5, column 6).

2 Ibid. See also the *Warren Journal*, Oct. 1, 1886 (page 3). Shipman's arguments concerning the indictment do not appear in the transcript, but they are addressed in detail in the Appellate Court's decision, reported in *New Jersey Supreme Court Reporter*, June term, 1886, under the caption Titus v. State (pp. 336-42). The appellate decision was rendered by the same Justice Beasley whose holding it was in the court below.

3 Minutes of the *Warren County Court of Oyer & Terminer Quarter Session*, vol. 3, page 346 et seq. See also *The New York Times*, Sept. 29, 1886 (page 5, column 6); *Washington Star*, Sept. 30, 1886; and *Warren Journal*, Oct. 1, 1886.

4 *Warren Republican*, Oct. 1, 1886.

5 *Washington Star*, Sept. 30, 1886.

6 Testimony of Augustus Dellicker (Transcript, 1-8/0011).

7 Testimony of John White (Transcript, 1-58/0098); Calvin Cutler (Transcript, 1-70/0120); Charles Seals (Transcript, 1-75/0129).

8 Testimony of Charles Reese (Transcript, 1-92/0159);

9 Testimony of Bridget Grogan (Transcript, 1-119/0209).

10 Testimony of Jesse Smith (Transcript, 1-201/0240).

11 Testimony of Stella Sliker (Transcript, 1-201/0354).

12 Testimony of George Beatty (Transcript, 1-226/0398).

13 Testimony of Mary Wright (Transcript, 1-234/0412).

14 Testimony of Agnes Wright (Transcript, 1-270/0475).

15 *The New York Times*, Oct. 1, 1886 (p.2, column 4).

16 Testimony of Annie Van Syckle (Transcript, 1-287/0504).

17 Testimony of Charles Munnich (Transcript, 1-319/0557). It is not known whether Munnich testified about Tillie's encounter with Frank Weeder next to the post office on the night of April 8. The newspaper accounts of the testimony fail to mention it and the pages of the transcript in which the encounter would have been related (334-337) are missing.

18 Testimony of Arturo Rivera (Transcript, 1-393/0681) and Harry Smith (Transcript, 1-420/0729).

19 Testimony of William Van Syckle (Transcript, 1-287/0504).

20 Testimony of James McMillan (Transcript, 1-446/0774).

21 Testimony of Harry Haring (Transcript, 1-461/0798).

22 Testimony of Dr. George Whitney (Transcript, 1-467/0807).

23 Ibid. at 1-469/0810.

24 Ibid. at 1-470/0812.

25 Ibid. at 1-402/0868.

26 Ibid. at 1-408/0876.

27 Testimony of Nathan Smith (Transcript, 1-433/0923).

28 Testimony of Elizabeth Ruckle (Transcript, 1-447/0947).

29 Testimony of Dr. John S. Cook (Transcript, 1-500/1039).

30 Testimony of Dr. Richard Cook (Transcript, 1-588/1191), Dr. Isaac Ott (Transcript, 1-572/1163) and Dr. Samuel Johnson (Transcript, 1-585/1185).

31 Testimony of Frank Bowlby (Transcript, 1-598/1208) and William Wieder (Transcript, 1-630/1263).

32 King and Bowlby's advertisements were carried regularly by the *Hackettstown Gazette*. The quotations here are from the *Gazette* of April 2, 1886.

33 Testimony of William Oseler (Transcript, 1-674/1338).

34 Ibid., at 1-682/1354.

35 Testimony of Niels Madsen (Transcript, 1-699/1384).

36 Testimony of Thomas Howell (Transcript, 1-726/1430).

37 Testimony of Peter Mead (Transcript, 1-754/1479).

38 Ibid., at 1-761/1496.

39 Ibid., at 1-808/1577.

40 Ibid., at 1-812/1584.

41 Ibid., at 1-816/1590.

42 Testimony of John McCoy (Transcript, 1-895/1727).

43 Testimony of George Van Campen (Transcript, 1-898/1732).

44 Testimony of Edward Zimmerman (Transcript, 2-947/1824) and Edward Fuller (Transcript, 2-951/1831).

45 Testimony of Isaac Baldwin (Transcript, 2-983/1886).

Chapter Five

1 *Washington Star*, Oct. 14, 1886 (page 1, column 2).

2 Justice Mercer Beasley's charge to the jury is a separate document appended to the trial transcript, located in volume two, beginning at Microfilm Index 2801; see also the *Washington Star*, Oct. 21, 1886.

3 Testimony of Rebecca Titus (Transcript 2-995/1906); testimony of Nettie Titus (Transcript, 2-1013/1937).

4 Testimony of Ralph Titus (Transcript, 2-1036/1977).

5 Testimony of Thomas Howell (Transcript, 2-1047/1996).

6 Ibid., at 2-1049.

7 Ibid.

8 Ibid., at 2-1052.

9 Testimony of Joshua Curtis (Transcript, 2-1053/2009).

10 Ibid., at 2-1054.

11 Testimony of William Drake (Transcript, 2-1056/2015); testimony of Nelson Drake (Transcript, 2-1083/2063).

12 Summation of Prosecutor Sylvester Smith (Transcript, 2-1454/2707, et seq.).

13 Testimony of Emma Titus (Transcript, 2-1129/2143).

14 Testimony of Jesse Bilby (Transcript, 2-1140/2160).

15 Testimony of George W. King (Transcript, 2-1159/2193).

16 Testimony of Charles Carpenter (Transcript, 2-1167/2207).

17 Testimony of Dr. J. Marshall Paul (Transcript, 2-1174/2214).

18 Ibid., at 2-1182.

19 Testimony of Dr. Comegys Paul (Transcript, 2-1190/2249); testimony of Dr. Henry Cox (Transcript, 2-1219/2300); testimony of Dr. Alva Van Syckle (Transcript, 2-1240/2338).

[20] Testimony of Dr. Comegys Paul (Transcript, 2-1213/2262 et seq.).

[21] Testimony of George Sherer (Transcript, 2-1262/2368).

[22] Ibid., at 2-1258.

[23] Ibid., at 2-1283.

[24] Ibid., at 2-1288.

[25] Testimony of Mark Dolan (Transcript, 2-1297/2438).

[26] Testimony of Dr. Joseph Wells (Transcript, 2-1347/2525).

[27] The prestige of the rebuttal witnesses contrasted drastically with the low social standing of witnesses Sherer, Dolan and Gray. Calling Dolan's veracity into question was Andrew J. Huntsman, a freeholder (Transcript, 2-1399/2618); impugning Gray and Sherer's reputations for truthfulness was John C. Chamberlin, a Justice of the Peace (Transcript, 2-1400/2619).

[28] *The New York Times*, Oct. 10, 1886 (page 2, column4).

[29] Testimony of Elizabeth Ruckle on rebuttal (Transcript, 2-1358/2544).

Chapter Six

[1] All quotations from the attorneys' closing statements in this chapter are from the *Washington Star* editions of Oct. 14 and Oct. 21, 1886. The official record of the four summations consists only of a small part of prosecutor Sylvester Smith's remarks (Transcript, 2-1458 through 2-1507, covering the afternoon of Monday, Oct. 11). A comparison of this fragment with the *Star's* account of it discloses that even if the latter is not a verbatim rendering it covers all the important points. It was decided for consistency's sake to use the *Star's* accounts of the other three summations, on the assumption that since all were published more or less side-by-side they were in all likelihood prepared with equal attention to accuracy. There is understandably a degree of risk in this approach, but it represents our best source for narrative purposes.

[2] The reference is to Psalms 57:12-13 (King James Version): "For it was not an enemy that reproached me; then I could have borne it; neither was it he that hated me that did magnify himself against me; then I would have hid myself from him; But it was thou, a man mine equal, my guide and mine acquaintance."

[3] *The New York Times*, Oct. 16, 1886 (page 2, column 2).

[4] *The New York Times*, Oct. 24, 1886 (page 3, column 3).

[5] The text of the decision appears in *New Jersey Supreme Court Reporter*, November term, 1886, as James J. Titus v. State. The summary states, in part: "3. A verdict in a capital case will not be set aside unless the irregularities committed by the jury be of a nature to raise a suspicion that they may have prejudiced the prisoner."

[6] *The New York Times*, Jan. 25, 1887 (page 1, column6); see also the *Hackettstown Gazette*, Jan. 28, 1887.

[7] Ibid. The Clerk of the Court recorded the sentence in the minutes somewhat more dramatically: "The prisoner again being placed at the bar to receive his sentence, the Court do order and adjudge that he be taken to the jail from whence he came and there safely keep [sic] until Thursday, April 24, 1887 between the hours of 10 A.M. and 2 P.M. of said day and that he be hanged by the neck until he be dead dead dead."

[8] Both the *Hackettstown Gazette* of Jan. 28, 1887, and the *Minutes of the Court of Oyer & Terminer* for Jan. 24, 1887, recorded the appointment of twelve witnesses to the execution. According to the minutes, such witnesses were required by statute to be residents of Warren County, liable for grand jury service, and "respectable persons," two of them physicians. Dr. J. Marshall Paul, Titus' physician and a witness for the defense, was one of the two selected.

Chapter Seven

[1] *The New York Times*, Feb. 27, 1887 (page 7, column 2).

[2] *The New York Times*, March 24, 1887 (page 2, column 2); see also the *Washington Star*, March 24, 1887 (page 3, column 3).

[3] The first mention of a commutation was made in *The New York Times* of March 23rd (page 5, column 2), and refers to the event of March 22, but makes no mention of a confession as the underlying reason for it. The confession material appeared in the *Times* on the following day, March 24, but since the *Hackettstown Gazette's* Friday edition would have been on the presses on March 24, it seems certain that both newspapers finished the race in a dead heat.

[4] *Hackettstown Gazette*, March 25, 1887; *Belvidere Apollo*, March 25, 1887.

[5] *Hackettstown Gazette*, March 25, 1887.

[6] *Washington Star*, March 24, 1887 (page 3, column 3).

[7] *Belvidere Apollo*, March 25, 1887.

[8] *The Sun*, March 26, 1887, column entitled "Tillie Smith's Murderer."

[9] Ibid.

[10] Ibid.

[11] Hackettstown Gazette, Nov. 25, 1887.

[12] Letter from Peter F. Mead dated June 13, 1887, Document No. 5876.25.26 in the collection of the Hackettstown Historical Society.

[13] *The New York Times* of Dec. 28, 1904, devoted about one inch of column 4, page 5 to the event.

[14] *Hackettstown Gazette*, Dec. 30, 1904 (page 3, column3).

[15] Ibid.

Chapter Nine

[1] Testimony of Dr. Comegys Paul (Transcript, loc. cit.).

[2] Ibid., at 2-1217.

[3] Testimony of Mary Wright (Transcript, 1-239/0418).

Appendix

Order of witnesses as recorded in the bound volumes of trial testimony and as reproduced on microfilm.

Seq.	Witness	Date	Vol.	Starting at Page	Microfilm
	— FOR THE STATE —				
1	Albert Buell	29 Sep	1	1	0
2	Augustus Dellicker	29 Sep	1	8	11
3	John G. White	29 Sep	1	58	98
4	Calvin Cutler	29 Sep	1	70	120
5	Charles Seals	29 Sep	1	75	129
6	Charles Reese	29 Sep	1	92	159
7	Bridget Grogan	29 Sep	1	119	209
8	Jesse Smith	30 Sep	1	137	240
9	Calvin Cutler (recalled)	30 Sep	1	199	350
10	Stella Sliker	30 Sep	1	201	354
11	George Beatty	30 Sep	1	226	398
12	Mary Wright	30 Sep	1	234	412
13	Agnes Wright	30 Sep	1	270	475
14	Annie Van Syckle	30 Sep	1	287	504
15	Charles Munnich	30 Sep	1	319	557
	pp. 334-337 missing				
16	Arturo Rivera	01 Oct	1	393	681
17	Harry Smith	01 Oct	1	420	729
18	William Van Syckle	01 Oct	1	437	758
19	James McMillan	01 Oct	1	446	774
20	Theodore Henderson	01 Oct	1	456	791
21	Maggie Donovan	01 Oct	1	458	793
22	Harry Haring	01 Oct	1	461	798
23	Dr. George Whitney	01 Oct	1	465	857
	pp. 486-488 missing; irregular pagination				
24	Nathan Smith	04 Oct	1	433	923
25	Elizabeth Ruckle	04 Oct	1	447	947
26	Lewis Ayers	04 Oct	1	474	995

27	Jacob Deremer	04 Oct	1	494	1030
28	Henry Stoddard	04 Oct	1	497	1035
29	John S. Cook, MD	04 Oct	1	500	1039
30	Isaac Ott, MD	05 Oct	1	572	1163
31	Samuel Johnson, MD	05 Oct	1	585	1185
32	Richard Cook, MD	05 Oct	1	588	1191
33	Frank S. Bowlby	05 Oct	1	598	1208
34	William Wieder	05 Oct	1	630	1263
35	Jesse Baggot	05 Oct	1	657	1309
36	Catherine S. Smith	05 Oct	1	659	1312
37	Dr. William Oseler	05 Oct	1	674	1338
38	Bridget Clark	05 Oct	1	684	1355
39	Daisy Cook	05 Oct	1	688	1363
40	Mary Timmins	05 Oct	1	691	1368
41	Mary Burns	05 Oct	1	692	1370
42	Rosa Martin	05 Oct	1	695	1377
43	Mary Cummings	05 Oct	1	696	1379
44	Niels Madsen	05 Oct	1	699	1384
45	Jacob Shields	05 Oct	1	714	1411
46	Dr. Alden Martin	05 Oct	1	718	1418
47	George Thompson	05 Oct	1	719	1419
48	George McCracken	05 Oct	1	723	1425
49	Thomas B. Howell	05 Oct	1	726	1430
50	Peter F. Mead	06 Oct	1	754	1479
51	Dr. George Whitney (recalled)	06 Oct	1	880	1701
52	Ann O'Shay	06 Oct	1	885	1710
53	Katherine Grace	06 Oct	1	886	1712
54	Bridget McMahon	06 Oct	1	888	1715
55	Horace Stout	06 Oct	1	890	1719
56	John McCoy	06 Oct	1	895	1727
57	George Van Campen	06 Oct	1	898	1732
58	Augustus Dellicker (recalled)	06 Oct	1	900	1736
59	Edward Zimmerman	07 Oct	2	947	1824
60	Edward Fuller	07 Oct	2	951	1831
61	Jesse Smith (recalled)	07 Oct	2	979	1879
62	Isaac Baldwin	07 Oct	2	983	1886

— STATE RESTS —

— FOR THE DEFENSE —

63	Rebecca Titus	07 Oct	2	995	1906
64	Nettie Titus	07 Oct	2	1,013	1937
65	Wilbur Sutphen	07 Oct	2	1,035	1975
66	Ralph Titus	07 Oct	2	1,036	1977
67	Thomas B. Howell	07 Oct	2	1,046	1995
68	Joshua Curtis	07 Oct	2	1,052	2008
69	William Drake	07 Oct	2	1,056	2015
70	George Van Campen (recalled)	08 Oct	2	1,076	2050
71	Nelson Drake	08 Oct	2	1,083	2063
72	Mrs. Ralph Titus	08 Oct	2	1,129	2143
73	Benjamin B. Cook	08 Oct	2	1,136	2157
74	Jesse Bilby	08 Oct	2	1,140	2160
75	George W. King	08 Oct	2	1,159	2193
76	Charles Carpenter	08 Oct	2	1,167	2207
77	J. Marshall Paul, MD	08 Oct	2	1,170	2213
78	Comegys Paul, MD	08 Oct	2	1,190	2249
79	Henry M. Cox, MD	08 Oct	2	1,219	2300
80	Alva Van Syckle, MD	09 Oct	2	1,240	2338
81	George Sherer	09 Oct	2	1,256	2366
82	Mark Dolan	09 Oct	2	1,297	2438
83	George Gray	09 Oct	2	1,332	2499
84	Joseph H. Wells, MD	09 Oct	2	1,347	2525

— DEFENSE RESTS —

— REBUTTAL FOR THE STATE —

85	William A. Conover, MD	09 Oct	2	1,354	2537
				p. 1,355 duplicated	
86	Elizabeth Ruckle (recalled)	09 Oct	2	1,358	2544
87	Lewis Ayers (recalled)	09 Oct	2	1,366	2558
88	James A. Hummer	09 Oct	2	1,371	2576
89	Samuel Caskey	09 Oct	2	1,378	2580
90	William T. Osmun	09 Oct	2	1,380	2584
91	Peter D. Smith	09 Oct	2	1,381	2586
92	Dr. William McGee	09 Oct	2	1,385	2593
93	Peter Smith (recalled)	11 Oct	2	1,397	2614
94	Horace Stout (recalled)	11 Oct	2	1,398	2616

95	Andrew J. Huntsman	11 Oct	2	1,399	2618
96	John C. Chamberlin	11 Oct	2	1,400	2619
97	Dr. John S. Cook (recalled)	11 Oct	2	1,406	2630
98	Dr. Richard Cook (recalled)	11 Oct	2	1,408	2633
99	Dr. Samuel Johnson (recalled)	11 Oct	2	1,412	2640
100	Jesse Smith (recalled)	11 Oct	2	1,415	2645
101	John Norton	11 Oct	2	1,423	2660
102	Dr. William McGee (recalled)	11 Oct	2	1,428	2669
103	Dr. George Whitney (recalled)	11 Oct	2	1,430	2673
104	George Van Campen (recalled)	11 Oct	2	1,432	2677
105	John Sinerson	11 Oct	2	1,436	2683

— STATE AND DEFENSE REST —

Bibliography

Cummins, George W.: *History of Warren County, New Jersey.* New York, N.Y., Lewis Historical Publishing Company, 1911.

Custard, Leila: *Through Golden Years 1876-1943.* New York, N.Y., Lewis Historical Publishing Company, 1947.

Dale, Frank: *...By The Neck Until Dead.* Hackettstown, N.J., Hackettstown Historical Society, 1995.

Dalton, Ernest: *The History of Hackettstown.* Hackettstown, N.J., Hackettstown Gazette, 1953.

Friedman, Lawrence M.: *Crime and Punishment in American History.* New York, N.Y., Basic Books, 1993.

Honeyman, A. Van Doren: *Northwestern New Jersey, A History of Somerset, Morris, Hunterdon Warren and Sussex.* New York, N.Y., Lewis Historical Publishing Company, 1927.

Lee, James: *The Morris Canal, A Photographic History.* Easton, Pa., Delaware Press, 1983.

Nunn, Harold: *The Story of Hackettstown.* Easton, Pa., Correll Printing Company, 1955.

Nunn, Harold: *The People of Hackettstown.* Easton, Pa., Correll Printing Company, 1956.

Portrait and Biographical Record of Hunterdon and Warren Counties, New Jersey. New York, N.Y., Chapman Publishing Company, 1898.

Shampanore, Frank: *History and Directory of Warren County, N.J.* Washington, N.J., Shampanore & Sons, 1929.

Snell, J.B.: *Warren County.* 1880.

Wacker, Peter: *The Musconetcong Valley of New Jersey.* New Brunswick, N.J., Rutgers University Press, 1968.

Warren County Board of Chosen Freeholders: *Historical Sites of Warren County.* Belvidere, N.J., 1965.

Woodall, George: *Incidents of Student Life.* New York, N.Y., Nelson & Phillips, 1878.

Source Documents:

Death Certificate of Matilda Smith, Warren County, 1886. New Jersey State Archives, Trenton, N.J. on microfilm, Index #S25.

Letter from Peter F. Mead to the Common Council of Hackettstown, N.J., dated June 13, 1887, claiming the reward. Files of Hackettstown (N.J.) Historical Society, Document No. 5876.25.26.

Minutes of the Court of Oyer & Terminer, October 1886 through January 1887, covering details of the trial, conviction and sentence of James J. Titus. Office of the Clerk of Warren County, Belvidere, N.J.

Petition by citizens of Hackettstown to the Mayor and Common Council urging the offering of a reward in the Tillie Smith murder, dated April 19,

1886. Files of the Hackettstown (N.J.) Historical Society, Document No. 5877.25.26.

State of New Jersey, Census of 1885, microfilm copy. Collection of the Warren County Public Library, Belvidere, N.J.

State v. James J. Titus, original trial transcript, prepared by Knight & Gnichtel, Legal Stenographers, Trenton, N.J., 1886 (bound, two volumes, 1,507 pages). Rare Books Collection, New Jersey State Library, Trenton, N.J. Catalogued under the title "Trial of James J. Titus."

Annual Catalog of Centenary Collegiate Institute (1896-1897), New York, Eaton & Mains Press, 1896. From the collection of the Methodist Archive at Drew University, Madison, N.J.

Belvidere Apollo, Belvidere, N.J. (1886-1887), microfilm copy. Collection of the Warren County Public Library, Belvidere, N.J.

Hackettstown Gazette, Hackettstown, N.J. (1886-1887 and 1904), microfilm copy. Collection of the Warren County Public Library, Belvidere, N.J.

Warren Republican, Hackettstown, N.J. (1886-1887), microfilm copy. Collection of the Warren County Public Library, Belvidere, N.J.

The Express, Easton, Pa. (1886), microfilm copy. Collection of the Easton (Pa.) Public Library.

Washington Star, Washington, N.J. (1886-1887), microfilm copy. Collection of the Warren County Public Library, Belvidere, N.J.

The New York Times, New York, N.Y., (1886-1887 and 1904), microfilm copy. Collection of the Phillipsburg Free Public Library, Phillipsburg, N.J.

The Herald, New York, N.Y. (1886-1887), microfilm copy. Collection of the New York Public Library, New York, N.Y.

The Tribune, New York, N.Y. (1886-1887), microfilm copy. Collection of the New York Public Library, New York, N.Y.

The Sun, New York, N.Y. (1886-1887), microfilm copy. Collection of the New York Public Library, New York, N.Y.

The World, New York, N.Y. (1886-1887), microfilm copy. Collection of the New York Public Library, New York, N.Y.

National Police Gazette (issues of May 1, 1886, and Oct. 16, 1886), microfilm copy. Collection collection of the New York Public Library, New York, N.Y.

About the Author

Denis Sullivan grew up within shouting
distance of the crowds at Ebbets Field,
in the days before the Brooklyn Dodgers
left for Los Angeles. After moving to
Warren County, N.J. in 1984, he saw
the Tillie Smith monument in Union
Cemetery and determined to find the
story behind it. He and his wife Joan
have two daughters.

The Hall-Mills Murder Case

"The Minister and the Choir Singer" were found near lovers lane. The sensational murders were never solved. Attorney William Kunstler explores the facts. 344 pgs. **$16.95**

The Lindbergh Kidnapping — cartoon drama

Lost for 65 years! Found in a New Jersey barn! Original cartoon drama traces "The Crime of the Century." Fully colorized computer-repaired panels with notes. 36 pgs. **$4.95**

Lindbergh Newspapers

Time travel in a box! 11 re-issued local newspapers cover the "Trial of the Century." Rare photos. Depression-era ads are priceless! Great gift for history buffs, seniors and legal eagles. **$29.95**

The Lindbergh Case

Best book yet on the Lindbergh kidnapping and the "Trial of the Century." Depression-era mystery still fascinates millions. 27 illus. 469 pgs. **$19.95**

The Ghosts of Hopewell

Former FBI agent Jim Fisher revisits the Lindbergh kidnapping. His second book reviews the evidence and rebuts theories that Hauptmann was innocent or that conspiracies were involved. Hardbound. 200 pgs. **$19.95**

The Lindbergh Kidnapping — video

New documentary features Gen. Schwarzkopf, Reeve Lindbergh and others on the famous kidnapping and trial. The vintage newsreel footage alone is priceless. As seen on Court TV. **$29.95**

Lindbergh's Great Race — video

Many tried before Lindbergh soared to fame and fortune. Engaging documentary shows flamboyant fliers who sought the fabulous Orteig Prize. 90 mins. **$29.95**

See the back page for information about ordering books and videos.

The Indians of New Jersey

A boy shipwrecked in 1612 is captured by Lenape Indians. As he earns a place in the tribe, we learn their culture, lore and sense of humor.
351 pgs. **$14.95**

Traditions of Hunterdon

A classic is back! Facts and fancies — from where Washington slept to which ghosts roam the Sourland Mts! Must reading for local history buffs.
210 pgs. **$9.95**

Tales and Towns of Northern New Jersey

Folklore from the master — Henry C. Beck's vivid tales of back roads and small towns of yore.
349 pgs. **$16.95**

The Roads of Home

More tales of lost towns and legends by Henry C. Beck. His pages brim with outlandish characters.
270 pgs. **$15.95**

Smuggler's Woods

Amusing true tales of Jersey smugglers and privateers helping the cause of liberty.
322 pgs. **$18.95**

Folklore and Folklife of New Jersey

Our rich heritage of folktales, song, dance, architecture, the arts, crafts and festivals.
218 pgs. **$19.95**

This is New Jersey

New edition explores all 21 counties in this most surprising of the 50 states.
291 pgs. **$16.95**

See the back page for information about ordering your books.

The Ride to Pleasant Grove

A modern couple, repairing their rural Lebanon Township home, follow clues to learn about a pre-Civil War family on this same farm.
160 pgs. **$12.95**

Sketches of a River Town

A lively history of a river town tells the story of Frenchtown through the years. Many old photos.
92 pgs. **$7.95**

I Remember

Gloria Paleveda tells stories of her life growing up along the Delaware, in Frenchtown, early in the 20th century. Includes 18 old photos.
80 pgs. **$7.95**

History of Stockton

Attractive Stockton has feisty character and a lively history. Here's an account of 300 years in the tiny borough, complete with 58 rare old photos.
76 pgs. **$7.95**

Union Township: Rural Reflections

Local history and lore include the "Battle of Jutland," Civil War veterans and more.
300 pgs. **$25.00**

Wandering West Amwell

From Lenape villages to George Washington's look-out rock, there's much to learn in West Amwell.
233 pgs. **$15.00**

Hunterdon's Role in the Revolution

This large format, 88-page booklet describes scores of brave local men and women who fought to found a free nation. Many rare old illustrations.
$7.95

See the back page for information about ordering your books.

A Precious Place

Local naturalist Don Freiday spins his favorite tales of wildlife. An engaging flock of stories, whether you're in your tent or home by the hearth.
161 pgs. **$9.95**

Canoeing the Delaware

Updated edition details this beautiful river. Access areas, campsites, rapids, historic sites, canoe-rental and safety. Maps & photos.
244 pgs. **$16.95**

30 Walks in New Jersey

Windswept beaches, rolling hills, broad green river valleys await you. Walks rated easy through difficult, in time and miles. An updated, expanded classic.
243 pgs. **$14.95**

Guide to Flemington

Excellent illustrated tour of Hunterdon County seat's buildings and history. An engaging handbook on Victorian and Greek Revival gems.
198 pgs. **$8.95**

Flemington Children's Choir School — video

100th Anniversary Concert. Home-movie tape includes concert and alumni remembrances of the Choir School founded in 1896 by the two Miss Bessies.
90 mins. **$12.95**

Rookie Dad

Come along on a voyage of laughter and minor mayhem that we call a family. Humor by Rick Epstein.
183 pgs. **$7.00**
Signed hardcovers: **$10.00**

To place your credit card order, call 908-782-4747 ext. 603

D. H. Moreau Books

HUNTERDON COUNTY DEMOCRAT, INC.
18 Minneakoning Road • P.O. Box 32 • Flemington, N.J. 08822-0032

(Prices do not include sales tax or postage.)